Alfred Kroeber

Leaders of Modern Anthropology Series
Charles Wagley, General Editor

ALFRED KROEBER

by Julian H. Steward

Columbia University Press

1973 NEW YORK AND LONDON

Library of Congress Cataloging in Publication Data

Steward, Julian Haynes, 1902–1972.
  Alfred Kroeber.

  (Leaders of modern anthropology series)
  Includes selections from Kroeber's writings (p. 63)
and a select bibliography of his works (p. 133)
  1. Kroeber, Alfred, 1876–1960. I. Kroeber,
Alfred, 1876–1960. Selections. 1973.
II. Series.
GN21.K7S84   301.2′092′4 [B]   72-8973
ISBN 0-231-03489-X
ISBN 0-231-03490-3 (pbk)

Preface

✢ Alfred Louis Kroeber was the major figure shaping the history of anthropology during the first six decades of this century. His career was one of brilliant and continuous productivity. His professional reputation was second to none and he was warmly respected by his colleagues as the dean of anthropology. At his death in 1960, Kroeber's insatiable curiosity had not been curtailed, his scholarly writing had not slackened, and his zest for life was undiminished.

The fullness of Kroeber's life was manifest in many ways. He played a major role in developing American anthropology from the rather random endeavors of amateurs and self-trained men to a coherent academic and museum discipline. His contributions to knowledge included extensive ethnographic investigations in California, the Southwest, the Philippines, and the Great Plains; archaeological studies in Mexico and Peru; linguistic research, especially in California; theory of communications in the animal world generally; historical syntheses which often had world scope; and a large number of papers on the nature of culture.

Kroeber developed one of the world's great research museums and teaching departments of anthropology at Berkeley, California. As the impact of his influence was felt, kudos accrued to him. He was the recipient of five honorary degrees (Yale, California, Harvard,

Columbia, Chicago) and two gold medals, had honorary membership in sixteen scientific societies, and held offices in innumerable
professional organizations.

As I confront the task of writing his biography now, I am fully
aware of many difficulties I had not experienced in writing the obituary for the *American Anthropologist* (1961) and for the National
Academy of Sciences (1962). I had not attempted to assess the fundamentals of his thinking for I feared the risk of misplaced emphasis
and misinterpretation. This risk now must be taken, for even though
I was Kroeber's student and held him in very high esteem, I was
not his disciple. I write this volume in full recognition that some of
Kroeber's greatest achievements, especially in his contributions to
linguistics and his vast knowledge of history, are outside my own
field of competence.

A difficulty in appraising Kroeber's work is that it was cumulative
rather than identified with any single scientific discovery or hypothesis, such as those of physics or biology. His purpose in ethnographic linguistic, or archaeological, and, later, in historical studies
was set forth early in his career, even in his doctoral dissertation.

This book attempts to assess those qualities that made Kroeber
one of the major figures of anthropology, to characterize his scholarly
point of view, and to identify the influences that brought about this
view and his achievements. It is not a biography in the ordinary
sense nor is such a biography needed. His widow, Theodora Kroeber,
in her recently published (1970) *Alfred Kroeber, a Personal
Configuration,* has written fully and compassionately about his life.
I have drawn heavily upon this account, especially the portion pertaining to his family background, and the early years before I
knew him personally.

I knew Kroeber first when I became a graduate student in 1925. I
believe I know reasonably well his principal interests and emphases.
My own approach to anthropology entailed a search for causes
whereas Kroeber's was more interested in distinguishing characteristics of cultures.

Theodora Kroeber's biography has confirmed my conviction that
Kroeber experienced few crises or points of major decision in his

professional life. The German-Jewish intellectual community of New York, in which he was reared, made his dedication to learning, with a strong inclination toward the humanities, inevitable. This was enhanced by the private training which he received prior to college, and by his family life, which made intellectual and esthetic matters all pervasive.

Kroeber might have chosen some field of scholarship other than anthropology, and, in fact, very nearly took up studies in English literature, but after he was committed to anthropology, his view of culture and the position anthropology should take in viewing culture and more broadly civilizations unfolded with what seems to me complete inevitability. It is these aspects of Kroeber's life and character with which I seek to deal.

An assessment of Kroeber's work is difficult, partly because of the great variety of subjects that it covered and partly because Kroeber repeatedly denied being a scientist. He considered himself a natural historian, interested in the "humanistically tinged" aspects of culture. He referred to anthropology alternatively as "natural history" or as "natural science," though he seemingly preferred the former designation.

Why and how Kroeber acquired this orientation toward cultural studies is, I believe, fundamentally traceable to his earliest childhood experiences and subsequently to the influence of Franz Boas, his teacher, and to contemporary trends within anthropology generally.

This book is divided into three parts. The first describes Kroeber's family background, the nature of the childhood influences he experienced, and his college training. This is based largely upon Theodora Kroeber's biography. It happened that I first knew Theodora Kroeber in 1926 when we both took a seminar under Kroeber, though she had known him slightly a few years earlier. They were married in 1926. After that time my friendship with the Kroebers continued.

The second part presents my own appraisal of Kroeber's intellectual achievements. This differs in certain particulars from Theodora Kroeber's assessment and somewhat also from that of others who knew Kroeber intimately in a professional capacity. It seems to me that the many honors which accrued to Kroeber by the end of his life were attributable to the sheer magnitude of his knowledge of cultures, history, and language, which extended beyond the scope of conventional anthropology.

The third part consists of quotations of various lengths from Kroeber's own writings. These excerpts are intended to state in his own words the views I have emphasized in Part II, though other persons may, and many doubtless will, consider that different excerpts from his nearly 600 books and articles are more representative of his professional thinking.

To objections to my own analysis in Part II and to my selections for Part III, I can only plead that, owing to the great stature of the man and the vast variety of interests on which he wrote, there is of course room for considerable difference of opinion.

I view Kroeber's greatness—a term I use advisedly—as a result of a combination of circumstances. His primary interest in natural history and the humanities was obviously the inevitable product of experiences during his childhood and youth, as I attempt to show. Having chosen anthropology as a profession, the empirical approach to language and culture taught by Boas was highly congenial to him. Scientific or explanatory formulations found no place in Boas's comparative approach. The term "scientific" is used to designate precise scholarship and constant empiricism rather than a purpose or method. Kroeber, however, added an interest in prehistory and history to the Boas approach. Through the years, Kroeber's keen mind, vast erudition, and extraordinary ability to express himself, together with the predominance of a relativistic view of culture, made him incomparable.

In preparing this volume I gratefully acknowledge the generous help of Theodora Kroeber and Robert Heizer. The latter published an obituary in *Man* (June, 1961) and in *Masterkey* (July–September, 1961). I am indebted to Dell Hymes, who wrote a penetrating analysis of Kroeber's linguistic contributions, one of his major fields, for *Language* (Vol. 37, 1961), and to John H. Rowe, who made an excellent assessment of Kroeber's archaeological work for *American Antiquity* (Vol. 37, no. 3, 1962), and who wrote an obituary for

The Teocintli (No. 25, 1961). Rowe, in addition to listing Kroeber's principal archaeological publications in his appraisal of Kroeber in *American Antiquity*, published with the cooperation of Anne Judith Gibson a nearly complete bibliography of Kroeber's works in the *American Anthropologist*.

This bibliography was reproduced with my biographical memoir of Kroeber written for the National Academy of Sciences in Vol. 36, 1962.

Other important publications on Kroeber included memorial remarks at the University of California at Santa Barbara by Ralph L. Beals in 1962 and an article in the *Encyclopedia of Social Sciences* (1968). In 1936, Carl Alsberg, a childhood friend, recounted Kroeber's early years and recorded insights into the man for the foreword to the Festschrift published in honor of Kroeber's sixtieth birthday. In the present volume I have relied heavily on these publications, but I could not hope to describe Kroeber as a man with the completeness of one who was his lifelong friend or one who was his wife for thirty-four years.

Theodora's title, *A Personal Configuration*, aptly indicates not only the nature of the man but also one of his unrelenting scholarly strivings. In her Preface she says, "Kroeber being Kroeber, there was, I began to discover, no unpatterned miscellaneous way of writing meaningfully of him. To tell anything of him is to become aware of the pattern and the configuration which are at the heart of the person and the personality . . . Kroeber was more of a piece than are many of us, his life pattern deeply cut, clearly outlined" (p. vii).

Contents

Contents

Alfred Kroeber

PART I

Biographical Sketch

FORMATIVE YEARS

The factors that shaped Kroeber as a man and scholar must be judged from miscellaneous writings and notes about him. Kroeber left no autobiographical material, and he had an aversion to writing about himself. There are, however, occasional notes and interviews on phases of his professional career. Above all, there is the beautifully written biography by his widow, Theodora Kroeber, and there are reminiscences of his youth written by his lifelong

1

friend, Carl Alsberg. Kroeber's contributions are best viewed in terms of his deep conviction that living and growing things—organisms, individual persons and their minds, and cultures—are indivisible wholes which must be understood in terms of developmental tendencies without dissection into components, and without search for particular causes. Kroeber's childhood and youth, his emergence as a scholar, and his adult years of professional endeavors exhibit a rare continuity. There are no discernible intellectual dislocations and doubts, no dramatic discoveries, and no sharp turning points. The childhood experiences led naturally into the professional career which consisted of a continuous amplification of a lifelong purpose. The only period of uncertainty about his professional future was the years devoted to psychoanalysis after 1918.

The background of the man and scholar was the German-Jewish upper middle class society of New York City in which intellectual, esthetic, and scientific interests and professional aspirations were a matter of course. This society of German families was a fairly close-knit and extensively intermarried group, it shared a very special German-derived American culture (though none of its members thought of it as non-American), and it produced a disproportionate number of eminent scientists, writers, lawyers, and other professional persons. Family life, child training, and private tutoring followed the German pattern.

Kroeber's parents were upper middle class Protestants of German ancestry. Grandfather Kroeber had come to the United States in 1840 when his son, Florence Kroeber, was ten years old, and he fought in the Civil War. Alfred Kroeber's mother, Johanna Muller, was American born to a German family which also produced many distinguished persons, including Herbert Muller, and a Nobel laureate in genetics, the late Herman Muller.

Florence and Johanna had four children, all of whom acquired a scholarly interest, especially in natural history. Although Kroeber's younger brother died at an early age, his sisters went on to achieve prominence in education in the New York school system.

Alfred, the oldest, was born in Hoboken, New Jersey, on June 11,

2

1876, but his family moved to lower Manhattan when he was still very young. Florence was a prosperous importer, especially of clocks, who was able to maintain a household of servants and to send his children to private tutors and schools, and yet he did not impose a commercial profession upon them. During Alfred's childhood, upper Manhattan was given over to considerable farm land and to Central Park. (The urban portion of lower Manhattan subsequently spread northward.) This fact gave ready opportunity for Kroeber's private tutor to indoctrinate him in natural history through field trips to the countryside.

The nature of Kroeber's childhood is recounted in Theodora Kroeber's biography, and illuminating items appear in the sketch by his friend, Carl Alsberg, in the introduction to the Festschrift presented to Kroeber on his sixtieth birthday in 1936.

A combination of factors was obviously critical to Kroeber's development. First, his family was bi-lingual, although German was the language used at home. He later remarked when discussing his interest in linguistics that he was introduced to Greek and Latin during his childhood, which stirred an enduring interest in linguistics. He observed that, as a school boy, he had been intrigued by the forms, or grammars, of language but had preferred Greek and Latin because English was too simple.

Another important factor was that at the age of seven or eight, after having been taught at home, he was placed under a private tutor, Dr. Hans Bamberger, whom he shared with six other children. This vigorous German not only taught the three R's but also made geography lessons vivid through providing his students views from Brooklyn Bridge, he stimulated their interest in natural history by means of collecting expeditions in Central Park, and he so excited his students about classical history that, during summers on Long Island, they erected forts to fight ancient battles, such as the siege of Troy. Kroeber then became enrolled in the Ethical Culture School, which attempted to supplant religious doctrine with natural philosophy as a basis for ethical judgments. The natural history exposures had a profound effect, for Kroeber and his friends made and classified collections of stones, plants, and other specimens with which they tended to litter their homes, though Kroeber's mother did not object.

Finally, the Kroeber children were, according to their age, permitted to take their places at the dinner table and, equally importantly, to accompany their parents to operas and concerts, which remained a major interest and recreational outlet throughout Kroeber's life. Kroeber's home environment apparently adhered to a strict regime, without, however, stifling his spontaneity. His formal schooling continued in the German pattern. He was sent to Sach's Collegiate Institute, the equivalent of grammar school and high school, modeled on the French lycée or German gymnasium, which prepared boys for college. Except for a year spent at the Gunnery, a private boarding school in Connecticut, to recoup his health, which was considered to be somewhat fragile, he continued there until he entered Columbia College in 1892, at the age of sixteen.

His formative years established the fundamental characteristics of the man and scholar; his vast range of interests with special emphasis on natural history, a love of language, extraordinary esthetic perceptiveness, and a strong sense of workmanship or willingness to do well all the grubby little chores required of first-rate scholarship. Carl Alsberg described the young Kroeber as shy and reserved but more than most boys an independent thinker and a dissenter.

Kroeber's achievements also clearly stemmed from his parents. Opportunity and circumstances alone could not make a Kroeber. His parents bequeathed him his high intelligence, quick comprehension and grasp of problems, and his retentive memory.

CHOOSING A PROFESSION: COLLEGE YEARS

Kroeber's transformation to adulthood was more an unfolding of latent tendencies than the agonizing choice of a career which is so common today. He attended Columbia College, although his father had had serious business reverses, and eventually received his Ph.D. at Columbia University in 1901.

As an undergraduate student he formed an attachment to three other young men, including Carl Alsberg. These students were highly talented and deeply interested in the humanities. They became the nucleus of a discussion group which devoted much time to art, literature, and other humanities, and they published a new paper, "The Morningside," which barred no subjects, including criticism of the University. Kroeber majored in English, taking his A.B. in 1896 and an M.A. degree in 1897, for which he wrote a dissertation on the heroic English play. He continued to be an instructor in English for two more years, 1897–99.

This group of friends made what seems to me a highly significant request of Columbia University for the teaching of culture history. Boas was appointed to the faculty only in 1896. Livingston Farrand, later President of Cornell University, gave a course in primitive cultures and another in material psychology; W. V. Ripley, a specialist in railroad economics and known for his book, *Races of Europe*, taught a course in physical anthropology, but Kroeber apparently had taken none of these courses. His interest in culture was such, however, that the group, presumably owing to Kroeber's instigation, recommended that culture history, rather than political history, be taught. It is said that the appointment of James Harvey Robinson to the faculty resulted partly from this recommendation.

This is the first indication that Kroeber was interested in culture history rather than historic personages and episodes. This theme was to remain dominant in his scholarly work and to characterize his later decades. One wonders at the source of this interest. It was not courses given at the university, but one must remember that, as Kroeber himself was to observe later, anthropology was not new. It had been a museum subject long before it was introduced to universities. Moreover, the British had a vigorous group of anthropologists who wrote largely on cultural evolution during the nineteenth century. This included E. B. Tyler, the so-called father of anthropology who first published in the 1870s. In America, the Ethnological Society had been founded in 1842 and the Bureau of American Ethnology in 1872. L. H. Morgan, the cultural evolutionist, had published basic works during the 1870s. An enquiring mind such as Kroeber's was undoubtedly aware of the distinctive cultural approach of anthropology, though the recommendation

5

that Columbia University introduce a course in culture history was hardly derived from any of these authors, who dealt almost exclusively with primitive cultures. Kroeber's role in this insistence at such a young age is surely a case of rare comprehension and foresight, since anthropology has only recently become interested in modern culture and its history.

Regardless of where Kroeber acquired his ideas on culture history, he was enticed into anthropology by Franz Boas through the humanistic and lingustic features of primitive man. German born, Boas had drifted into anthropology and ethnography from geography. He was employed by the Royal Ethnographic Museum of Berlin before coming to the United States. An early visit to Baffin Land interested him in the folklore and language of the Eskimo, and he later served on the faculty of Clark University and as curator of the American Museum of Natural History before being appointed to Columbia University in 1896.

Quite by chance Kroeber took Boas's seminar on American Indian languages which was given at his home. A small group of Central Eskimo brought to New York City by Robert Peary was the main attraction, and curiosity led Kroeber to attend. The seminar met around Boas's dining room table. Kroeber, however, became so enchanted that he shifted his major interest and efforts to anthropology, and went on to become Boas's first Ph.D. in 1901, and the second in the United States.

From 1899 to 1901 Kroeber was affiliated with the American Museum of Natural History, where, under Boas's auspices, he had the opportunity to study Indians of the far west, including the Arapaho, who were then in Oklahoma, and several tribes of the Great Basin.

Kroeber's Ph.D. dissertation was twenty-eight pages long, on Arapaho art. In it, he clearly foreshadowed his basic point of view. The intellectual foundations of the thesis will be discussed subsequently.

We must digress here to another facet of Kroeber's thinking. When Kroeber entered anthropology, Carl Alsberg raised interesting doubts about such a career, which disclose a real, though covert, idealism in Kroeber. Alsberg, who chose a career in chemistry, argued against Kroeber's going into a subject so "vague, inchoate, and intangible" to which Kroeber replied that "a result in chemistry or physics . . . was not likely to affect men's thinking and to make for progress in the only way that was worth while . . . to free men intellectually. The confused thinking about religion was perhaps the most important bar to man's freedom." In subsequent years, Kroeber continued to be interested in religion, though much of his analysis treated it objectively and analytically, as he dealt with other facets of culture. His interest in man's progress surfaced from time to time, to be treated in the same way.

Kroeber's interest in cultural values many years later was more than a humanist's view of styles or contexts. He treated the questions of objective or scientific criteria of progress quite explicitly in several papers, and yet he eschewed programs of research aimed at social reform. Apparently he wished to create a perspective and to destroy ethnocentric thinking without committing himself to problems of human welfare.

FIRST PROFESSIONAL YEARS

In 1900, at the age of twenty-four, Kroeber accepted his first professional position in California. He was to remain in California for the balance of his life, and although he retired in 1946, he always returned subsequently to his home in Berkeley whenever possible between guest lectureships and conferences.

Kroeber's first position was with the California Academy of Sciences in San Francisco. Here he resided and worked under David Starr Jordan, then President of the Academy, for $80.00 per month. Earlier part-time curatorial work for the American Museum of Natural History had afforded some preparatory experience for this position. An Anthropological Museum, and later a Department of Anthropology were subsequently created at the University of California, and Kroeber always found museum work congenial. On various occasions he called attention to the fact that anthropology had grown up as a museum subject long before Boas's academic teaching, and that it had acquired two of its three fundamental characteristics during this association. First, its concern with collections and its natural history classifications; second, its humanistic component, which dealt especially with esthetics, lent themselves to exhibits. The third component, social science, was added later, after anthropology was introduced to universities, when it became associated with political science, sociology, economics, technology, psychology, and geography.

He was attracted to California, as Theodora Kroeber points out, less by the grandeur of its mountains than by its riverine and estuarian tribes. The Yurok Indians of the lower Klamath River and the Mohave Indians of the lower Colorado River became his special subjects of study. In fact, Kroeber continued field work among them all his life, and he gave seminars on them while at Columbia University after his retirement. He invited old Yurok friends to visit at his home in California.

Kroeber found California a congenial and fertile field, especially for his interests in linguistics and ethnology, for the state has within its borders more different languages than any other area of comparable size in the country. Most of the main linguistic stocks of North America are represented there, including Athabaskan, found mainly in Canada; Algonkian, which occurs in the eastern United States; and Shoshonean, which is found in the Great Basin and Southern California. Many of its languages which had not previously been classified were eventually assigned a place in the major language stocks owing to the efforts of Kroeber and his colleagues. Kroeber did not neglect ethnography nor archaeology, however, and he constantly accumulated ethnographic information and museum specimens.

After a year, the California Academy of Sciences found itself unable to pay Kroeber's salary and a modest sum to support field studies. Kroeber very fortunately had formed a lasting friendship with Mrs. Phoebe Apperson Hearst, the mother of William Randolph Hearst. Mrs. Hearst had begun to acquire archaeological collections from Greece, Rome, Egypt, and Peru, but she had no place to keep them. She arranged with Benjamin Ide Wheeler, President of the University of California, to pay Kroeber's salary for five years to care for her specimens and to be an instructor in a new Department of Anthropology. A special building to house the Department and Museum of Anthropology on the Berkeley campus was planned. Meanwhile, a store house two stories high and sixty or eighty feet square was built of corrugated iron on the campus to house statuary. An interior balcony at the second floor level provided office and classroom space. The remainder of the collections were placed in a special museum made from an unused building of the Hastings Law College at the Affiliated Colleges in San Francisco. Thus, the Department of Anthropology began its distinguished career in 1901.

For many years, however, Kroeber's duties were mainly curatorial, and he resided in San Francisco, commuting to Berkeley only to meet classes. When Mrs. Hearst lost some of her fortune, the dream of a single building for both the Museum and Department in Berkeley was deferred, and in fact it did not materialize until 1959, the year before Kroeber's death, when a combined Alfred L. Kroeber Hall, Robert H. Lowie Museum of Anthropology, and an Art Museum were finally constructed. Kroeber attended the dedication in May, 1960.

Kroeber was made Assistant Professor in 1906, Associate Professor in 1911, and Professor in 1919. Frederick Ward Putnam of Harvard University was chairman of the Department, devoting part time to it in an advisory capacity for several years.

For many years, the Museum remained in San Francisco as did Kroeber's residence, but the Department was in Berkeley, to which Kroeber commuted until the teaching chores became too great.

When Kroeber accepted a position at the University of California, Mrs. Hearst guaranteed Kroeber and Pliny Earl Goddard, who collaborated with Kroeber, each an annual salary of $1,200 per year. Frederick Putnam was nominally in charge in an advisory capacity, for he could visit California only occasionally and for brief periods. After Putnam retired, Kroeber took complete charge of the Museum and the Department. He soon enlisted the help of Edward Winslow Gifford, who had been trained as an ornithologist, as curator of the Museum. Gifford remained in this position until his death. He

9

had learned a great deal of anthropology and gave some of the courses. Some years later Kroeber engaged T. T. Waterman, an extremely popular lecturer, who gave the introductory course. It was said that he had an enrollment of some 800 students, which was truly remarkable for a university which at that time numbered not over 5,000 students.

Kroeber's main addition to the Department, however, was Robert H. Lowie, who had come as a visiting professor but whom he engaged in 1918 on a permanent basis. Lowie, like Kroeber, was a Boas student. Subsequently Ronald Olson, a student of Kroeber's, was hired to teach the introductory course and others, and then Theodore McCown, another of Kroeber's students, was engaged because of his special knowledge of physical anthropology obtained in Europe under the postgraduate guidance of Sir Arthur Keith.

Kroeber added an archaeologist to the staff when Robert Heizer was employed in connection with the California Archaeological Survey. In 1946, John H. Rowe was engaged. An omission from the staff was a specialist in linguistics. This is the more curious in view of Kroeber's own interest in the subject. Kroeber had given instruction in linguistics to Carl Vogelin and later to others, including Dell Hymes, but the full rounding out of the faculty was extremely slow.

During his first twenty years in San Francisco, Kroeber had suffered several traumatic experiences which apparently nearly deflected his interest from anthropology to other matters. These were the loss of his wife, the death of the famous Ishi, the so-called wild Indian, and an ear infection which had caused frequent serious dizziness and which resulted in permanent loss of hearing in one ear.

The great earthquake of 1906 fortunately did little damage to the Museum which adjoined Golden Gate Park. Kroeber's own residence in a hotel, however, was completely demolished by fire.

A few months after the earthquake Kroeber married Henrietta Rothschild. Henrietta was the descendant of German Jews, but the marriage to a gentile caused no concern among her relatives. The marriage began auspiciously. Henrietta was talented and musically inclined, but fragile. Within a few years she developed tuberculosis, and died in 1913. This was a deeply tragic experience for Kroeber, who did not remarry for thirteen years. Then he married Theodora Krakaw Brown.

Not many years after Kroeber's marriage occurred the experience involving Ishi, the extraordinary Indian discovered and captured in the foothills of the Sierra Nevadas. The fascinating story of Ishi is the subject of a separate book published by Theodora Kroeber (1967). Ishi, who was the last survivor of his tribe, had been reported as a "wild" man. He was finally apprehended by white men, but fortunately Kroeber was notified and, together with T. T. Waterman, arranged to have Ishi come to San Francisco and live at the Museum, where he received especially considerate treatment. Ishi was the source of much valuable information for a number of years and his superb techniques of chipping obsidian points was transferred to glass, of which he made many beautiful specimens. Ishi, however, contracted tuberculosis and died in 1916.

Meanwhile Kroeber had begun to suffer from what proved later, though then undiagnosed, to be an ear infection. The symptoms were quite alarming, even causing him to fall in the street on occasion. Eventually he recovered from this illness, though with a complete loss of hearing in his left ear. He had noticed that the illness was more acute at times of emotional distress.

In 1915–16, Kroeber took his sabbatical year and traveled rather widely in Europe, including Vienna, where he came in contact with Freud's school of analysis. The following year he engaged Robert H. Lowie to fill in for him at the University of California while he worked in New York. While there, he was analysed by a student of Freud's. The psychoanalysis helped Kroeber resolve his emotional difficulties, but it produced the first major choice Kroeber had to make in his professional career. When he returned to California, he himself became an analyst with such success that by 1923 he recognized that he must choose between the profession of psychoanalysis and that of anthropology. With considerable regret he gave up psychoanalysis and devoted himself exclusively to his teaching and museum duties, which by this time had been firmly secured on the Berkeley campus.

Many persons have been surprised that his experience with psychoanalysis did not deeply affect his view of culture. It has always seemed to me that precisely because of Kroeber's preconceptions of the nature of culture and because of his deep knowledge of psychoanalysis he kept the two separate. During the 1930s when, following the Abram Kardiner influence on so many anthropologists and the emergence of the so-called culture and personality school, Kroeber was able to cling steadfastly to his previously established views of culture, that culture is a strictly superorganic phenomenon which is not reducible to an organic level. The experience served mainly to enrich his vocabulary.

Except for the illness that led Kroeber to psychoanalysis, he devoted the first twenty years of his career pretty strictly to the languages, folklore and ethnology of California. During this period his publications on languages often in co-authorship with Pliny Earl Goddard, Roland B. Dixon, and others, consisted mainly of linguistic and folkloristic studies, largely published in the University of California Publications in American Archaeology and Ethnology, which he had founded in 1903. The principal exception to California studies was his work in 1915 among the Zuñi, where he not only did linguistic studies which included the processes by which a child learns the language, but also archaeological studies. He developed the idea of seriation in archaeology, perhaps through exchange of ideas with A. V. Kidder. (This was the means of ascertaining the relative age of different surface sites by comparing the percentages of sherds of different types.)

Kroeber's vast accumulation of ethnographic data in California during this period was assembled in the *Handbook of the Indians of California*, finished in 1918, and revised in 1923 when it was published as a Bulletin of the Bureau of American Ethnology.

In 1924 Kroeber visited Mexico to pursue archaeological studies and he laid the foundation of his continued interest in the area. His main interest, however, was in Peru, owing largely to the Max

Uhle collections obtained for Pheobe A. Hearst. Uhle had excavated grave lots with such precision that Kroeber, assisted by his students, W. D. Strong and Anna Gayton, prepared the material for publication.

TRANSITION TO BERKELEY

When the Museum of Anthropology was in San Francisco, Kroeber maintained residence in the city, visiting Berkeley mainly to meet classes. His teaching obligations were not great although Kroeber met his classes faithfully. The enrollment had been limited, and one of his first classes on the American Indian was attended by only six students, but interest in anthropology increased until today Berkeley has perhaps the largest graduate student body in America.

While still resident in San Francisco, Kroeber gave graduate work. The Department was understaffed and was to become more so in 1908–9 when only Kroeber carried the teaching chores.

The growth of the teaching department marked the gradual transition from San Francisco to Berkeley for Kroeber. The Museum of Anthropology had remained at the Affiliated Colleges which required a very long commuting trip. The Museum was nearly an hour by street car west of downtown San Francisco where Kroeber continued to reside, and the trip to Berkeley was about an hour by ferry and street car.

During his San Francisco period Kroeber did not relinquish his interest in the California Academy of Sciences, although he had resigned his original position. In 1903 he had become secretary and during many years he published annually on the progress of the anthropology collections.

Kroeber's obligations on the campus, however, grew sufficiently great that in 1917 he moved to the Faculty Club in Berkeley. Some years later an old engineering building was vacated on the campus, ironically near the Hayward fault, which Kroeber obtained for a museum, and the collections were moved into it. It was more a research museum than a place for exhibits.

In 1926, when he married Theodora Krakaw Brown, a widow with two young sons, he bought a beautiful redwood house in north

Berkeley. This remained his home henceforth. At first he built a room adjoining the house which was entered from the outside because it was intended as a place where his psychoanalytic patients could visit him privately, but since his practice was all but abandoned by this time he converted it into a study, which was a great convenience when he and Theodora had two small children of their own.

Soon thereafter, the Kroebers bought a place, Kishamish, in Sonoma County for summer vacations, where guests frequently included informants from northern California tribes.

By the 1930s Kroeber continued to produce monumental books which appeared rather unexpectedly in view of their great volume and importance, as he rarely discussed work in progress. *Natural and Cultural Areas of North America* (1939) was one of these and *Configurations of Culture Growth* (1944) another. During the early 1930s Kroeber devoted several years to the culture element lists. A large number of persons were employed collecting lists from most tribes or divisions thereof west of the Rocky Mountains and he entered into it himself with great vigor. I suspect, however, that eventually he recognized the comparative futility of the project, which he abandoned rather abruptly.

The first Ph.D. under Kroeber at the University of California in anthropology was awarded Samuel A. Barrett, who wrote on the Pomo in 1908. The next went to W. D. Strong in 1926. By 1930, seven degrees had been awarded. Between 1931 and 1946, the year of Kroeber's retirement, he gave twenty-five. These were predominantly in ethnology, because Kroeber had not believed in appointing staff members who specialized in archaeology or linguistics, which he considered to be simply parts of cultural studies. By 1960, the Department had given fifty-seven degrees, many of them the result of specialization in the different fields of anthropology.

After the United States became involved in World War II Kroeber directed the newly created Army Specialized Training Program (ASTP) at the University of California, although he had been eligible to retire at the age of sixty-five in 1941. The strain and frustrations of this new work brought on a serious heart attack and for some time it was uncertain whether he would survive. He recovered in 1946, the year when he was required to retire, and in time to go to England to receive the Huxley Medal of the Royal Anthropological Society. The paper he delivered upon this occasion was entitled *The Ancient Oikoumene*, and it consisted of an enumeration of the main differences between the eastern and western hemispheres in their cultural achievements. This award was especially remarkable because British anthropologists had been highly critical of American anthropology and had accorded this honor to very few.

After 1946, Kroeber was free of University duties, though he retained his residence in Berkeley. He was in great demand to teach wherever and whenever he could find time. He taught first at Columbia University, then at Harvard, again at Columbia, and also at Yale University, the University of Chicago, and Brandeis University, together with lecturing at several other places. Although he did not engage in extended field trips he maintained interest in his beloved Yurok and Mohave to the end of his life.

He had somehow found time in 1948 to make a further revision of his *Anthropology*, which now appeared as a 1,000-page work covering the major aspects of anthropology and including also the points that Kroeber himself had developed in previous years. Many of his efforts after his retirement were devoted to attendance at conferences which became increasingly numerous. For example, the Wenner-Gren Foundation had organized a world conference in New York in 1952, which Kroeber guided and summarized. The final day was memorable in that Kroeber followed his doctor's orders to rest for an hour after lunch while the hundred odd delegates wandered around in the stifling heat awaiting his summary. The Foundation purchased a castle at Burg Wertenstein in eastern Austria where Kroeber organized two conferences, the last just before his death, on "Horizons of Anthropology."

Kroeber's interest became more sharply focused on modern civilizations during the 1950s, perhaps stimulated by his frequent visits to Europe, although anthropology by this time was paying somewhat greater attention to the contemporary world. The Center for

15

Advanced Studies in the Behavioral Sciences had been founded at Stanford, California, and Kroeber was one of the first anthropologists to become a fellow. He was also one of the few who attended a second time and in these periods he wrote some of his definitive ideas on the relation of anthropology and history.

In 1956, Kroeber served as expert witness for the plaintiffs in the Court of Claims who were the California Indians who sued the government for reimbursement of old claims. Previously, he had always avoided governmental matters, and it seems to me that his participation on this occasion was rather helf-hearted.

Among the symposia which Kroeber was invited to conduct was that at the centennial of Darwin's *Origin of Species* held in Chicago in 1959. The evolution of cultures was treated by a somewhat strange assortment of persons. It included Sir Julian Huxley, who regarded cultural evolution simply as an extension of biological evolution and who was fairly dogmatic in his beliefs. It also included an ethnobotanist, Herman Muller, who regarded such things as floraculture in Indonesia as a genetically determined trait, and who took this occasion to proselytize for his constant theme, the deleterious effects of certain human marriages, and Gordon Willey, an eminent archaeologist from Harvard, who had never previously written on or as far as I know given serious thought to cultural evolution. Finally, it included Leslie White and myself, who presented our previously formulated views which, however, had little connection with the views of the other participants. Kroeber took this occasion to honor Darwin largely by substituting the term evolution for history.

Perhaps Kroeber's outstanding achievement during the 1950s was in writing final formulations of the problems presented by the relationship of anthropology and history, which his fellowship at the Center for Advanced Studies gave him time to do. Interestingly, an anecdote concerning Kroeber during his stay at the Center was his reply to a lavish introduction before speaking to a group. He said that the way to gain fame was to live beyond the age of sixty, after which fame automatically accrued. This was, of course, not literally true, since most scholars in their seventies and eighties drift into a period of non-productiveness. In Kroeber's case, however, it was very true, since he continued to expand and explain his interests in writing to the very end.

Subsequent to his heart attack he took very good care of himself and continued to be highly productive. His productivity did not consist of any sharp break with his former thinking, except that he devoted himself more completely to problems of the history of civilizations and to the effects of industrialization in changing the modern cultures of Europe and America, and a renewed interest in linguistics stimulated in part by research on animal communications. In fact, a work on contemporary European history had been planned shortly before his death; also he outlined in rather condensed and cryptic form periods of western cultural development. This work was published posthumously under the title *A Roster of Civilizations*. His most important work, however, consisted of a number of essays which were published in 1966 under the title *An Anthropologist Looks at History*. This work, which is his final statement, belongs no less to history than to anthropology. It is a measure of Kroeber's true greatness; for very few anthropologists have transferred the methods of comparative ethnography to modern civilized societies.

The years had not appreciably slowed Kroeber's endeavors nor dulled his interest in his work. Whatever one may think of the fundamentals of Kroeber's point of view, which lasted consistently throughout his life, his forays into the comparative history of civilizations and his delineation and discussion of the problems pertaining thereto, constitute a lasting contribution to the world of scholarship. His zest for activity continued to the very end.

In the summer of 1960, following a Wenner-Gren Conference, Kroeber and Theodora were vacationing in Paris when suddenly one night Kroeber had a final heart attack, thus ending eighty-four years of incredible productivity.

KROEBER THE MAN

All who knew Kroeber are unanimous in their acclaim of his great personal charm. Whether they knew him as guests in his home or in other relationships, their reaction to him was similar. Kroeber's appeal lay not in any effort to be affable but in his quiet attention to and interest in everything a person had to say. He was always interested in any new ideas one wished to express, and he was fascinated by gossip. He always listened quietly, interjecting appropriate and pointed queries from time to time. If the conversation tended toward gossip, Kroeber allowed it to flow freely. If, however, he was trying to settle a more serious point he deftly directed it through his comments.

As a judge of persons Kroeber was no worse than many and far better than most. On rare occasions he made errors in his assessment of certain individuals but usually he corrected them in the end. Kroeber had a sense of loyalty to those he had supported, which perhaps outran judgment and might be attributed to an innate conservatism, also manifest in certain scholarly matters, which he was very reluctant to change.

During my graduate years at Berkeley a group of graduate students, together with certain other persons, had formed the habit of foregathering in the home of Jaime de Angulo. This group was known as the North Berkeley Gang. Whereas Lowie and Gifford attended the occasional festivities of this group, Kroeber, so far as I recall, was never present. He gently warned us, however, to be careful of our behavior lest the university learn of it and we get into trouble.

Kroeber controlled his subordinates gently but firmly. It must be remembered that as time moved on he headed not only a growing department but also a fairly active research museum, both of which made considerable demand upon his time.

I never ceased to marvel that he could carry on his professional chores so effectively and at the same time produce so many massive volumes as well as monographs and papers, all of which he wrote in longhand. He also was a very successful father to four children, Clifton and Theodore, his stepchildren, who requested, and were granted, the right to be called by his surname, and Carl and Ursula, children of his marriage to Theodora. Part of his success is attributable to Theodora, who took care of the children, assisted by her aunt who lived with them after their marriage. His time was fairly clearly allocated. Kroeber found time to associate with his children, depending upon their age and comprehension, but he had a study at home readily available for escape from domestic affairs and it was equipped with a good library to use in pursuing his scholarly work.

In understanding his highly successful arrangement of his life one must remember first that, as all of us agreed, he was an extraordinarily smoothly functioning, well integrated person who appeared to have no serious inhibitions or conflicts, and, second, that Theodora made an ideal wife. He was fifty years old when they married, but thanks to Theodora he adapted with ease to the wholly new regime required of the head of a household.

Some of the fundamental patterns that Kroeber carried into his domestic life clearly seemed to stem from his own childhood experience. Theodora described his home as a German type. His father, unlike many German-Americans, however, earned his living through commerce, rather than through scholarly endeavors. He was tolerant of the children's interests and activities but apparently made little effort to direct them. On the other hand, his mother, a Muller, was extremely tolerant of the confusion inevitably created by his natural history interests and collections and the home laboratory paraphernalia such as Bunsen burners, collections, and other impedimenta that must have littered the house to some degree. Kroeber grew up with several household maids in attendance, and his own children were cared for by Theodora and her aunt, who served the younger children their dinner on trays in their rooms, rather than impose them on Kroeber. As the children grew older they, as Kroeber had done, participated in family dinners, and Kroeber always found some time to devote to the entire family. This was notably true at Kishamish, the summer house, where recreational facilities were installed and where fairly virgin woodland as well as chaparral was accessible. At any event, it is clear that all four children grew up with extremely high regard for Kroeber.

Kroeber's education made a profound and lasting impression on him. After speaking of the influence of the School of Ethical Culture on Kroeber, Theodora quotes him as saying, "One other factor was a permanent influence: the unalloyed respect which this environment had for learning and the arts and the premium which it put upon their cultivation. They were not something compartmented, a segregated specialty of the few, but things of daily experience, of constant contact. Not everyone became a scholar, an artist, a practitioner of a learned profession, but everyone lived in the atmosphere of association with them. The most gifted slid easily into the status of such a career, the others maintained the association and attitudes. This value for enlightenment may have been slightly reinforced in some Jews by a transmuted carry-over of the fetish of rabbinical learning. Essentially, however, it was the carry-over of the Europe of Voltaire which the founders of America of necessity largely escaped, in spite of the genius exception of Franklin. The form which molded Carl Alsberg (and Alfred Kroeber, of whom Kroeber was writing) was the mid-nineteenth century German facies: the mellow golden sunset of the German civilization of Kant and Goethe, translated to a late afterglow among congenial and harmonious American institutions."

Interestingly, Kroeber did not become a creative artist, poet, author of novels, or musician, though many of his closest friends achieved great distinction in various fields of creative arts and learning. Kroeber was, in the deepest sense, rather an analyst, a commentator and critic of the arts and humanities achieved, not only by others in America but, as his anthropological horizons expanded, those produced by primitive and civilized societies throughout the world. His canvas expanded until it became world-wide. His genius lay in an uncanny ability to identify the aspects of the achievements of any culture that were most significant and to make them explicit to others.

He approached the variety of world cultures because of their intrinsic interest; a preconceived plan which ascribed a priori importance to various aspects was quite lacking. As he frequently said, "I am interested in phenomena, not in causes."

Although Kroeber had been reared as a liberal, like most of his German-Jewish contemporaries in New York, I rarely heard him express an opinion on political events. Perhaps the principal com-

20

mentary on this score is that his sons grew up to be political liberals. He was cautious in holding to what appeared to be a fairly rigid hierarchy of values. His Department, as it affected himself and his family, came first. Next were political matters of the state and finally the nation, as they seemed to influence the University and through it the Department.

This hierarchy of values was, perhaps, a manifestation of his deep distrust of matters that in recent years and in a broader sense have become applied anthropology. He always admonished his students to stay out of governmental programs designed to solve Indian problems, and he himself became involved in the Indians' Court of Claims cases, vital as these were to the Indians' interests, only on the occasion of the Indians of California versus the United States government. This attitude toward applied social science quite clearly was part of a larger conception of the role of anthropology.

In departmental matters, Kroeber was always meticulously fair but sometimes surprisingly direct. Professor Robert Heizer sent me a transcript of letters from Kroeber to a field worker engaged during Kroeber's early years at Berkeley. The worker had consistently failed to send in an accounting of himself, and Kroeber wrote vigorously and frequently to call the failures to his attention.

One evening, while I was preparing the manuscript for *Petroglyphs of California and Adjoining States,* I had no typewriter and therefore dropped into the Departmental secretary's office to use her typewriter. Kroeber happened to arrive and gently admonished me that the secretary would probably be quite perturbed at having her typewriter used by someone else.

Kroeber was frequently called on to give his opinion of the suitability of various people for positions. In these matters he was always fair but it seemed, on occasion, that his caution was slightly in excess of the demand: that is, he always spoke very frankly of the proposed candidate so that his recommendations were usually heeded, but on occasion he pointed out the person's shortcomings in ways that were not altogether appropriate.

Kroeber's opposition to the reorganization of the American Anthropological Association in 1946 astonished me at the time and seemed to be a clear example of his extreme conservatism. Through the end of World War II, by which time all other professional organizations had been streamlined to function effectively, the Association had retained its early loose organization. It functioned only to publish the *American Anthropologist* and to elect as President the oldest living member who had not been so honored. Qualifications of membership, responsibility of the president and council, publication policies concerning the *American Anthropologist* vis-à-vis the other anthropological journals that had come into being, and above all, a means of responding between annual meetings to current crises were wholly neglected.

A new constitution was drawn to correct these needs and circulated among members, prior to the 1946 Annual Meeting. Kroeber and half a dozen other persons, however, were very insistent in their opposition. He apparently wanted the Association to remain as it was, a collection of scholars, who would avoid the pitfalls of applied anthropology, and he wrote me that this would be equivalent to "slugging the Association in the jaw and leaving it in the corner to die."

Kroeber's attitude was incomprehensible and the new constitution was overwhelmingly adopted. Within the past few years, however, I begin to see Kroeber's point. Little did I foresee at the time the Pandora's box that would be opened. The Association has passed one resolution after another on matters that most of us approve personally and that, in fact, we have accepted without question, but that do not constitute the essence of scholarship and cannot be supported scientifically; for example, political discrimination against minority groups, equal rights for women, equal treatment of homosexuals, opposition to the Vietnam war, and many other causes. Few of these can be justified or condemned on scientific grounds.

My lasting impression of Kroeber is shown in the photograph in the frontispiece. The "beard," a name by which many referred to him, was a neatly trimmed professional beard that he had cultivated in his early days.

PART II

Thought

THE FOUNDATIONS OF KROEBER'S SCHOLARLY THOUGHT

After his death in 1960, Kroeber received unstinted praise for his role in American anthropology. He was variously described in articles and obituaries by Dell Hymes, John H. Rowe, Ralph L. Beals, Robert Heizer, Earl Count, and many others as one of the greatest anthropologists of the twentieth century. His impact on anthropology has been lasting and to a large extent continues.

The extent of Kroeber's influence stemmed not only from the sheer brilliance of his mind and his prodigious and continuous output, but from an extraordinary facility in writing. Kroeber dealt with all branches of anthropology and made outstanding contributions to all of them. He recognized problems long before most of his colleagues, and where a satisfactory answer seemed impossible, he was the first to spell out the nature of the problem and the considerations relevant to the conclusions. Upon many occasions, I thought I had framed a new problem, only to find subsequently that Kroeber had already published on it.

A highly distinctive characteristic of Kroeber's thinking was his interest in the history of civilized societies, both ancient and modern. This interest extended largely beyond the interests of the so-called anthropologist proper. Although contemporary anthropologists deal with modern industrial cultures, none approaches the civilized societies in the same way as Kroeber. Indeed, according to trends in the past few years, the approach has become one of dealing with practical problems and their solutions, a matter that Kroeber carefully avoided throughout his life. Rather, he dealt with the kinds of history and the views of history that have been represented by such persons as Spengler and Toynbee, but he employed a strictly cultural approach.

Kroeber's endeavors were aided by an incredible fund of knowledge which was so great that one constantly wonders how he came by it. He truly managed to keep abreast of the greatly increasing output of work in the field of anthropology and at the same time to keep informed about the essential work in the allied social sciences, particularly in sociology, on which he wrote several incisive criticisms. The sheer volume of his output is the more incredible in view of the fact that he wrote only in longhand, and yet was able to produce at fairly short intervals such works as the *Handbook of the Indians of California, Configurations of Culture Growth,* and *Cultural and Natural Areas of North America.*

To these qualities of greatness must be added Kroeber's great longevity and his sustained creative output up through his last summer. From the time of his retirement from Berkeley at the age of seventy, until his death at the age of eighty-four, Kroeber's writings became somewhat more diversified. He was frequently requested to organize symposia and to summarize them.

The demands on his time in later years were so great that he had to carefully ration himself, largely because of health. Kroeber continued to publish research started many years earlier, and this research included such items as a California language or mythology.

Finally, it should be stressed, Kroeber had an extraordinary facility in writing. His choice of words was so apt that his meaning was rarely misunderstood. On the occasions when he revised or republished on a subject it was to introduce amplifying ideas rather than to clarify meaning. A characteristic of Kroeber's style was his extensive use of semicolons and colons. When an editor once protested such usage he replied that without such punctuation devices his sentences lacked topography. It is a style to be admired.

A biography would be quite incomplete without an attempt to identify the fundamentals of his thinking and to trace their origins, for Kroeber had remarkable self-consistency. His scholarly achievements were clearly rooted in his character and total behavior, and seem to have emerged from his youthful experiences.

One can only hope for partial success in such an endeavor, however, for the sheer magnitude of his writings evidences an omnivorous curiosity about all fields of anthropology, history, and indeed all fields of learning, as well as a philosophical orientation which led him to examine and to interrelate the assumptions and methods of these fields. The characterization put forward in the following pages can only be tentative and provisional, for the basic themes of Kroeber's thought recurred throughout most of his writings. An appraisal of his achievements by others will almost certainly have different emphases than I have given.

Selections from Kroeber's writings reproduced in Part III were chosen with some difficulty from the great diversity of subjects about which he wrote. A striking characteristic of Kroeber's work is its enormous attention to detail, which shows Kroeber's willingness to explore intensively all aspects of his problem.

The basis of Kroeber's point of view may be called the natural history of culture, with strong emphasis on the humanistic features. That is, Kroeber's main endeavor was to identify the distinguishing features of each culture and to assign them to categories based on the procedures of natural history, but he was wary in drawing conclusions about such a classification because he thought the dominant feature of each, a position of cultural holism, was a means of characterizing the entire culture.

Although virtually all anthropologists think of anthropology as a science, Kroeber expressly repudiated the value of a scientific method in the study of cultural phenomena. This was the natural outgrowth of his own interest in the humanities and of his comparative indifference to such features as social structure, technology, political organization, and cultural ecology, and also of his frequently repeated statement that anthropology had long been a museum study before it became an academic subject. Although Kroeber founded one of the great anthropology departments of this country, where he taught from 1901 to 1946, he constantly pointed out that anthropology was not originally a science and that it became so only after its association with other social sciences in the context of universities. The emphasis upon the natural history component, that is, the characterization of culture, pervaded all of his writing and it is interesting to note that a summary of his views, *The Nature of Culture*, published in 1952, introduces the volume with a chapter taken largely from his doctoral thesis of 1901 in which he sets forth his basic thinking and argues against a scientific approach.

Kroeber impressed students and colleagues by the volume and erudition of his writing. He was the author of nearly 600 articles, book reviews, and books, a number of which exceeded one thousand pages in length. Among these was the revised edition of *Anthropology* published in 1948. Although originally published in 1923 in far more modest form as a textbook, its sheer size has made it less practical as a textbook in subsequent years. Enquiries among students have revealed that they and contemporary anthropologists have the utmost respect for Kroeber but many are not entirely clear as to which of his achievements they admire. Some have said that they find his works, especially *Anthropology*, a valuable source of information. It should be noted, however, that, as the years passed, Kroeber tended to repeat in revised or even rewritten form previous articles, but his *Nature of Culture*, a work of 430 pages, contains thirty-two articles of which only a few are new. The others are reprints or revisions of previously published articles, the earliest from 1901.

A reader of Kroeber's works can start at almost any point and find the essential features of his views. As he developed new ideas he summed them up in subsequent works so that failure to read the totality did not leave one in ignorance of his thinking.

Kroeber was clearly "of a piece" (as Theodora Kroeber wrote of him), not only in the intergration of his personality but in the inner consistency and, in fact, inevitability of his scholastic thinking.

Today, reviewing Kroeber's writings, I note a basic and undeviating point of view which may be reduced to two major components. The first of these was his primary insistence upon characterization of the salient aspects of any culture. The second was the classification of cultures in categories which, in effect, is comparable to a natural history procedure. In addition to characterization and classification, Kroeber introduced additional elements which are somewhat peripheral to the first two: a strong historical sense and a view of cultures as a superorganic phenomenon.

Kroeber's two principal orientations were derived not only from his childhood background and interest in natural history but also were derived from or reinforced by his teacher, Franz Boas. The extent of Kroeber's genius, which lay in his absorbing interest in the history of civilizations with written records, was by no means shared by Boas, and remained, and indeed still remains, largely distinctive of the man. Also, Kroeber's early insistence on dealing with the superorganic, which, following Herbert Spencer, he distinguished from the organic and inorganic levels of the organization of phenomena, was also his own. In later years, however, his interest in the superorganic diminished although he never repudiated it.

By the same token, Kroeber did not deal in causes or explanations, of which he was always suspicious, although he was interested in any attempts by others in this direction.

27

The inevitability of Kroeber's point of view, I think, arises from the nature of his own experiences. He was indoctrinated as a child in a basically natural history procedure, which, though interrupted by forays into English literature in which he took a master's degree in college, was subsequently resumed under Boas with whom he took a seminar in linguistics. From the time of his doctoral dissertation, and indeed throughout his entire career, there seems to be a basic similarity, which stresses the interflow of cultural phenomena from one period or epoch to another and from one area to another. His thesis dealt with a long debated problem about art: namely, whether geometric art represented realistic elaborations of conventional forms or whether conventional forms were derived from realistic forms. He characteristically took a middle ground, concluding that Arapaho art showed that art forms, like other aspects of culture, displayed growing changes from one kind of art to the other and that no general explanation was possible. This general point is carried through in his subsequent work, such as *Cultural and Natural Areas of North America,* written in 1939, and *Configurations of Culture Growth,* published in 1944.

Kroeber's basic procedure, therefore, was one of a description of the salient features, whatever they might be, of any culture. Owing to the interrelatedness of the different aspects of culture none of these features could be clearly, or with certainty, related to others. This point of view, it seems to me, clearly developed from his interest in linguistics. Among the many unrelated linguistic groups in the world it has never been shown, and rarely suggested, that the distinctive form, grammar, or structure of any language was traceable to a cause. The most that could be done with linguistics was primarily on the descriptive level, and afterwards the assignment of languages to taxonomic categories or taxa, without any reference whatever to causes.

A related aspect of this assumption and procedure was Kroeber's strong belief that any culture be viewed holistically, that is to say, that all aspects of the culture be taken into account and evaluated. Although the term holism was not in vogue in Kroeber's early days he later employed it freely, for it expressed his basic view about the nature of cultures.

Kroeber was, in effect, totally in accord with Boas in considering that the most characteristic and distinguishing aspect of any culture had to be determined empirically, and that the salient features might differ in each case. The desire to compare cultures thus led to an effort to contrast cultures, which became known as cultural relativism, a view which predominated for many years, and to a certain extent still prevails in anthropology.

Cultural relativism entailed a contrastive approach to cultures, which Kroeber extended to historical civilizations, though in the case of the latter he amplified and refined this approach with supplementary considerations. Underlying Kroeber's cultural relativism was great attention to what he frequently referred to as style and pattern.

In an essay written during 1958, concerned largely with historical civilizations, Kroeber states that he is concerned with seeing how far "the concept of style can profitably be applied to the concept of civilizations viewed as wholes. A style may be provisionally defined as a system of coherent ways or patterns of doing things." He goes on to give the derivation of style from *stylus*, an instrument used in writing, and likens style, therefore, to individuality in writing. He points out that "with lapse of time the word has come also to denote a social or historical phenomenon, the manner or set of related patterns, common to the writers or musicians or painters of a period and country." This point is developed further in *An Anthropologist Looks at History*. It is notable that in this context, as in most other contexts, he comes very close to humanistic expressions of style, and that in his fundamental attitude toward culture he describes himself as a "humanistically-tinged natural historian." The impression throughout his work is that humanistic considerations are never far below the surface and that frequently they are expressly the focus of attention in the criteria used to characterize cultures. Again and again, the major characteristics of culture were stated to be such aspects as art forms including monumental architecture, religious concepts, and other humanistic features.

The second set of concepts characteristic of Kroeber, unlike the first, were not inseparably interrelated. The historical dimensions of cultures were added principally during his studies of recorded civilization; although Kroeber always pointed out that such dimensions were implicit but rarely ascertainable owing to the rather flat picture of history that was necessarily the only way of viewing history in ethnographic studies which lacked written records. Despite this, Kroeber projected the historic depth backward in time into prehistory, especially after World War II, when an enormous amount of effort was devoted to archaeology and the field of archaeology unfolded so as to include the beginnings of civilizations, as well as the more elaborated forms during florescent or classical periods.

In addition, Kroeber never really relinquished his insistence on the superorganic nature of cultural phenomena, even though in the 1930s the culture and personality school burst quite suddenly upon the country. The latter view was not in conflict with cultural relativism. Indeed, by its claim that adult personality was established during infancy it became an additional prop of the concept that any culture tended, according to the normative view of culture, to perpetuate itself, and thereby to resist change.

Kroeber shared his two-fold goal of describing and classifying with his teacher, Boas. All, or most, anthropologists have considered or spoken of anthropology as a science, but it is important to distinguish between several equally valid meanings of science. Anthropology is a subject that deals with rigorously documented facts, especially with empirically obtained field data, but this empiricism does not, per se, permit the arrangement of its phenomena in causal relationships. That is, it does not allow it to view the differences stressed by cultural relativity so as to recognize cross-cultural or recurrent similarities of function and causality. It is, in fact, in retrospect, basically a position of cultural relativism, a position that regards each culture as unique in its totality, even though culture elements are shared in different degrees, and therefore not amenable to cross-culturally valid explanatory formulations.

Kroeber repudiated a search for causality on the grounds that only history could disclose cultural origins and the constant interflow of different lines of cultural development. Especially, he saw such efforts to recognize causality as identical with the search for cultural origins. It is true that the nineteenth-century cultural evolutionists were no less concerned with origins than with cultural sequences. It does not follow, however, that causality is concerned primarily with origins, as Kroeber states in his *Nature of Culture*, especially in the chapter dealing with anthropology as a science, with functionalism, and with Leslie White and cultural evolutionism. It is difficult to see why cross-cultural process, whether it is abstracted from synchronic similarities or from diachronic resemblances which involve varying time depths, need be brushed aside as concerned with origins and therefore incapable of disclosing causality.

This view prompted Boas to devote an enormous amount of effort to studies of physical anthropology as well as language and culture in order to provide an empirical basis that exposed the fallacy of the so-called unilinear evolution of the last century. This nineteenth-century view was fundamentally based on an orthogenetic interpretation according to which all cultures were caused by the same genetic factors, and tended to evolve in the same direction; for this the basic explanation was a tendency toward progress and different cultures could be placed in an evolutionary niche according to cross-cultural similarities. Kroeber was in complete accord with this view, and because he accepted Boas's conclusions regarding unilinear evolution and its implications for cultural or linguistic evolution he did little first-hand research on physical anthropology with the purpose of giving further support to Boas's views.

Kroeber, however, gave the Boas view various emphases that were distinctly his own. He paid great attention not only to the distinctive characteristics of each culture and language but also to its humanistic implications. He considered culture holistically, that is, as a complex of patterns in which each was colored by its dominant and usually humanistic aspects. Because he considered each culture holistically, it was entirely legitimate, from his point of view, to range over the very wide spectrum of possible cultural emphases and search for a different one as the dominant characteristic in each case. This view gave Kroeber unlimited scope for characterizing each culture in different terms.

Kroeber paid far more attention to the diachronic aspects of culture, that is, to the historical aspects of culture change, than did Boas, whereas Boas was interested in culture history, though in his work and largely in his lifetime the cultures of primitive societies, since the American Indian, had little verifiable historical depth, he devised age-area studies by which a history of sorts was inferred from culture distributions. Kroeber developed this to its ultimate potential in his element distribution studies. Kroeber, also, was interested particularly during his latter years in the problems arising from the study of civilized societies, that is to say, of nations and cultures with written records. This had expanded his view of culture enormously and largely distinguishes his scholarly endeavors from those of other anthropologists. A projected study, never undertaken, was to deal with contemporary industrialized societies.

Kroeber repeatedly justified his distinction between scientific and cultural studies, by which he meant historical studies, by pointing to differences in the organization of phenomena. At first, in 1917, he borrowed Herbert Spencer's distinction between the superorganic or cultural, the organic and the inorganic, and insisted that a scientific or explanatory method was applicable only to the two lower levels. Sapir objected to the concept of the superorganic, and a lively exchange of papers in the *American Anthropologist* followed. Many years later Kroeber modified his scheme after psychological studies had begun to pervade anthropology and distinguished mainly the sociocultural, the psychic or psychological, the organic and the inorganic, the psychic being an intermediate level between organic and superorganic phenomena. By this time the culture and personality school which had been foreshadowed by Sapir had developed in the United States. Kroeber's reasoning, though intricate and not always clear, was substantially the same as during the early years. In a paper called "So-Called Social Science" (1936) he lumped together the efforts of sociology, economics, political science, and other social sciences as largely motivated by the efforts to improve human affairs and as therefore not truly scientific but also not historical, and outside the scope of anthropology. The concept that cultural studies are on a level of their own, which cannot be explained by organic or genetic factors, had the advantage of destroying racism as well as the early orthogenetic basis for cultural evolution. It did not, however, truly dispose of the possibilities of scientific or causal formulations between phenomena in the other social sciences, which, though perhaps predominantly oriented toward human betterment or problem solving, are by no means entirely devoid of scientific principles. Various types of British social anthropology known collectively as functionalism are similarly disposed of, as neither historical nor scientific. An outstanding case where a causal or explanatory formulation fails, that is, one in which cultural phenomena are clearly not related to causes, is linguistics, where causes have yet to be found although structures have changed and definitely diverged from one another. The nearest approach to postulating causes in linguistics is where diffusion, if diffusion can be lumped under causes, explains many lexical and phonetic and possibly some structural features.

It was unnecessary to introduce the concept of a psychic level in supporting the argument against causality because this level, like the organic level, has qualities common to all mankind, unless as by the nineteenth-century evolutionists and the modern racists, a genetic determinant of cultural behavior is postulated.

Subsequent sections deal with major aspects of Kroeber's thinking. I had presumed that those features that are an essential part of Kroeber's views could be segregated from those that are peripheral or in the nature of embellishments. I found, however, that one may start at almost any point of Kroeber's work and find the entirety of his scholarly views subsequently unfolded. For example, Kroeber's concept of levels seemed to be dispensible in his concept of cultural holism and his emphasis on history. This is not true, however, for he utilizes the concept of levels as justification of his total point of view.

Perhaps the most distinctive features in his thought are Kroeber's interest in the historical dimension of culture and the great prominence he accorded the humanities. These, it seems to me, skewed the nature of his scholastic contributions by excluding the most basic aspects of culture and by diverting attention from a methodology that could come to grips with the innumerable cases of causality contained therein.

LINGUISTICS

I think it may fairly be said that Kroeber arrived at anthropology through his interest in language and thence broadened out into ethnography, which Boas was only beginning to teach when Kroeber was a student at Columbia University. During his first two decades in California, 1900 to 1920, Kroeber did both linguistics work on the great diversity of California languages and ethnology, for he considered language but part of culture and did not sharply distinguish the two.

Kroeber's devotion to linguistics was truly remarkable in view of the history of linguistic studies in the United States. During the first four decades, or perhaps longer, of the twentieth century, language was definitely secondary to ethnological studies and teaching. To gain employment as an anthropologist one had to be primarily an ethnologist or archaeologist, and language skills were definitely incidental. Language was truly a second string to the bow, and at first not very important. Universities presented European languages, especially German, French, and others for which the student might subsequently have practical use, but linguistics as a subject that dealt with language, especially languages of primitive peoples such as those of the American Indian, was accorded little importance. For several decades the few exceptions were Franz Boas, one of whose main interests was primitive languages; John Swanton at the Bureau of American Ethnology; Edward Sapir, who taught at Yale University; and Kroeber. Perhaps this is part of the reason why Kroeber did not engage a full-time linguist during most of his period at the University of California. It is only in more recent years that linguistics has assumed its proper importance and, in fact, that it is taught either in departments of anthropology or in separate and usually relatively new departments of linguistics.

Many of Kroeber's efforts, however, were devoted to languages, particularly those of California, during his first twenty years there, and what teaching was done in the field was accomplished largely by Kroeber, himself. Dell Hymes, in his obituary of Kroeber (*Language*, vol. 37, no. 1, Jan.–March, 1961), has calculated that of a total of 460 papers published by Kroeber during his lifetime, 70 are at least partly devoted to linguistics. His linguistic work, moreover, falls into three phases: the first comprises the first twenty years of his professional life; the last the final ten years; and the remainder scattered through the intermediate thirty years.

Kroeber approached language as a natural history phenomenon, which is to say that the first task was to characterize it and subsequently to classify it. One must assume that the great importance that language played in Kroeber's thinking was partly influenced by his total thinking about culture. Linguistic structure may be described and classified but it cannot be explained by factors of another order. For this reason, it would appear, Kroeber was skeptical of any efforts to make explanatory formulations of any aspects of culture that involved other phenomena. In other words, the natural history of language was, in a sense, the ultimate goal.

Such a natural history, however, involved certain methodological considerations. The degree of similarity between linguistic structures showed, among other things, the probability of a common descent from a single language. Kroeber, in his study of California languages, however, showed that there were blocks of contiguous, though genetically unrelated, that is, structurally diversified, languages which shared other characteristics. Careful comparisons of these languages, which represented twenty-two of Powell's original classification of fifty-six North American language stocks, however, disclosed shared similarities other than structural ones. There were areas of contiguous linguistic groups that had in common lexical features, which Kroeber could and did estimate by a statistical approach. Also, there were phonetic resemblances. Kroeber apparently never reached a conclusion about whether any structural or grammatical features could be diffused from one language group to another as lexical and phonetic features obviously had been.

One of the most brilliant results of Kroeber's linguistic genius was an article published in 1909, "Classificatory Systems of Relationship." This paper pioneered an approach which has subsequently become known as componential analysis (Ward Goodenough, *Encyclopedia of Social Sciences*, Vol. 3, pp. 86–91). I do not recall that Kroeber ever used this designation, though he subsequently applied his approach to several languages including not only American Indian speech, but Chinese and others.

His initial study of kinship terms was answered a few years later by W. H. R. Rivers, who attempted to relate kinship terms to forms of social organization. Kroeber disagreed with Rivers's contention that these terms were simply a reflection of sociological categories in which individuals were placed. He suggested that the examples used were being drawn largely from European languages and contained many terms which were artificial and did not reflect certain basic characteristics which he had set forth.

Kroeber postulated that there were eight major categories for classifying relatives which were quite independent of any causality in the relationship of the speaker to the person designated. These categories were: generation; blood or marriage; lineal or collateral; sex of relative; sex of connecting relative; sex of speaker; age in generation; condition of connecting relative (*Nature of Culture*, 1952, p. 177).

In the same article Kroeber states: "If it had been more clearly recognized that terms of relationship are determined primarily by linguistic factors, and are only occasionally, and then indirectly, affected by social circumstances, it would probably long ago have been generally realized that the difference between descriptive and classificatory systems is subjective and superficial. Nothing is more precarious than the common method of deducing the recent existence of social or marital institutions from a designation of relationship." (*Nature of Culture*, p. 179.) In the introduction to this article he elaborated upon alternative approaches and their significance. He dealt extensively with L. H. Morgan, who used the classificatory influences to support his theory of unilinear evolution and progress. Rivers, who had worked mainly with Melanesian kinship, and Malinowski were cited as exemplifications of erroneous interpretations of the kinship of simpler tribal societies.

Kroeber clearly repudiated the causality between kinship systems and kinship terms implied by their interpretation and characteristically regarded his eight categories as purely linguistic phenomena which do not have any discernible causes.

His efforts in studying the factors involved in similarities between different languages in California constituted a model for North America generally, that has not been followed up by his successors.

At this point one can very appropriately quote Dell Hymes, one of America's leading linguists. An assessment of the great contributions of Kroeber to linguistics: "to understand fully Kroeber's historical work (his chief linguistic love) and to appreciate its value as a legacy, one must realize that each of the three main modes of historical interpretation for linguistic resemblances, genetic, areal, typological, had for him deep and lasting roots, the typological in his love for extrication of pattern, the areal in his ethnology, the genetic in his regard for its ordering power. All had a part to play in his concern for understanding through classification and context. The key to the shifts in priority of attention is that Kroeber, never a partisan of one mode of interpretation as against another, worked and recommended according to his sense of the weight of evidence as to the most productive direction of effort at a given time. He was quick to sense the diminishing return; at the same time, he seldom abandoned an interest, but kept it at hand (or let it lie fallow)" Hymes (p. 20). And further, "Kroeber's lasting contribution is almost wholly through his own substantive work and example, not as with Boas and Sapir, also through an impact on the descriptive method and on students trained by himself. Kroeber seemed always somewhat shy of the technical core of the 'philology' or linguistics as containing methods whose rigor he admired but with which he did not feel wholly conversant, or free, certainly not to the point of modifying them (his use of statistics is the one exception). He referred to himself as 'something of a philologist (= linguist).' In his review of Sapir's *Language*, he at most claimed no hesitancy with regard to a content he thoroughly knew, that of California Indian languages (*Handbook*, vi). In his hesitancy to claim the mantle of full-fledged linguist, he was but honest. His training in linguistic analysis came from a self taught pioneer well before the codification of descriptive methods, and his student contact with the comparative method was not, like Sapir's, first hand."

And finally, Hymes states, "Kroeber's massive contributions of data and interpretation show how greatly he felt the fascination of linguistics, despite his hesitancy. If any serious criticism can fairly be made of his California career it is that he did not see to the technical training of others during so much of the period in which he dominated the Berkeley department. In later years he insisted that no anthropology department could claim to be first rate without an active linguistic specialist, but not so in practice during his middle years."

ARCHAEOLOGY [1]

Kroeber did not consider himself primarily an archaeologist, and yet he ascribed more importance to historic depth or to diachronic studies of culture change than most early anthropologists. In this respect, Kroeber differed from Boas, who, though an originator of the age-area method of making historical inferences and reconstructions, was far less interested in history, especially of civilized societies, as a basic part of cultural studies than Kroeber.

Kroeber was trained as an ethnologist, with special interest in languages and folklore. At the turn of the century comparatively little was known of the prehistory of American Indian cultures. The almost universal interest in prehistoric artifacts had long been focused in the Archaeological Institute of America and expressed in museums. It was not until the mid-thirties that the Society for American Archaeology was established, and it was not really until after World War II that the attention of archaeologists became directed to the long development of early civilizations rather than principally to their more spectacular or classical manifestations or the eras of "florescence."

When Kroeber entered anthropology as a profession, therefore, archaeology was comparatively undeveloped both as to substance or content and in methodology. In both areas Kroeber made significant contributions.

Kroeber, however, paid great attention to developments in Old World prehistory as known through anthropology. The Eastern Hemisphere, of course, covered a much longer time span than the

---

[1] John Howland Rowe, in an obituary entitled "Alfred Louis Kroeber, 1876–1960," *American Antiquity*, 27 (1962), 395–415, has written an excellent appreciation of Kroeber as an archaeologist.

New World, and he summarized the data of Old World archaeology.

He was drawn to the field of American prehistory mainly because one of his earliest duties connected with Mrs. Hearst was to serve as custodian of the various collections of prehistoric objects she had accumulated from different parts of the world, including Uhle's pottery from Peru. Kroeber did not go to Peru until 1925 and 1926, which was about the time that he, with the assistance of his students, studied Uhle's collections in the California Museum.

Kroeber's first archaeological field work was undertaken rather incidentally while he was visiting Zuñi Pueblo in 1915 doing ethnography, published as *Zuñi Kin and Clan*. He became interested in the surface occurrence of potsherds at various sites around the Pueblo and developed the method of seriation by which, having dated certain of these, he was able to establish the relative age of the different types of pottery which he found. About the same time A. V. Kidder, in conjunction with Samuel Guernsey, was developing a cultural sequence starting with the Basket Makers and extending through the Pueblo cultures to modern times for the Southwest. Kidder, too, had devised seriation and it is not unreasonable to suppose that he and Kroeber had been in contact with each other during this time.

Kroeber did not do any field archaeology in California for many years but he became stimulated very early during his work in California by excavations at the Emeryville Shell Mound, an enormously deep and large refuse deposit, not far from Berkeley on the shore of San Francisco Bay. This was excavated in 1902 by Max Uhle who, while visiting California, worked under the pioneer archaeologist C. Hart Merriam. Kroeber focused his attention on problems of sequence for the Emeryville Mound whereby the cultures could be roughly divided into two main periods, the latter "neolithic" in character, and the former perhaps intermediate between "paleolithic" and "neolithic." Kroeber, who always adopted a skeptical view about new proposals, was reluctant to accept the time distinctions proposed by Uhle, for these would have violated the general impression that North American archaeology lacked any time dimension. I suspect, however, that Kroeber's reluctance to agree with Uhle was based on the very common assumption among North Americanists that a neolithic period, as distinct from a paleolithic one, could not be recognized as such in North America. That is to say, the dichotomy between paleolithic and neolithic persisted from attempts to equate American prehistoric cultures with those of the Old World, and Kroeber, like others, was naturally skeptical. In fact, as late as the 1930s [2] a few individuals were still attempting, though without success, to recognize similarities between the two hemispheres. Nels Nelson made a new excavation at Emeryville in 1906 but apparently did not resolve the differences between Kroeber and Uhle.

Although Kroeber did little archaeological work in California for some years, he gave, or arranged to have Nelson and later others give, a course on North American archaeology at Berkeley. He did not add an archaeologist as such to his staff until the late 1930s, then he engaged Robert Heizer to take charge of the California Archaeological Survey. W. D. Strong and I, who had both made a mess of our first archaeological field work, had pleaded with him to provide training in the basic techniques of archaeology. He did not respond, apparently on the assumption, which also applied to linguistic work, that both prehistory and language are parts of culture and that one can best learn about them through first-hand experience and reading. He later changed his mind and added John Rowe to the staff, about the time of his retirement.

After the interruption created by his psychoanalytic period Kroeber resumed his interest in New World prehistory through his studies of the Uhle collections. Kroeber had been greatly interested in Mesoamerica and the Central Andes as sources of culture elements for the remainder of America, but the Andes had received much less attention than Mexico. The Uhle collections included pots that were associated and well documented by grave lots but otherwise not related to one another in a chronological scheme. First in conjunction with W. D. Strong, who at that time was an undergraduate student in anthropology, and later with Anna Gayton, a graduate student, he undertook to correlate the Uhle collection. Although, as John Rowe

[2] In 1931, I attended anthropological meetings in Denver, where Dr. Renaud continued to proclaim the presence of pure paleolithic culture in America. That these meetings were opened with prayer I presume to be purely coincidental.

indicates, certain of Kroeber's historic sequences were proved later to be incorrect, he was generally correct in his interpretations, and above all, this served as a basis for a lasting interest in the Andes. The studies of the Uhle collection were published during the middle twenties. Meanwhile, however, Kroeber visited the Valley of Mexico in 1924 and the following year made the first of several field trips to Peru. Thanks to his knowledge of Peru, for many years Kroeber was invited to write interpretations of various general projects and collected endeavors concerning Peru.

In his approach both to the Valley of Mexico and to Peru Kroeber was almost exclusively concerned with ceramic styles and sequences rather than with the various other aspects of the civilizations which were so obtrusive as to be literally unavoidable and which he necessarily encountered and climbed over to arrive at the sites where he conducted ceramic investigations. This seems to me somewhat paradoxical in view of Kroeber's lifelong interest in the great civilizations of the world, among which Mesoamerica and the Central Andes were necessarily included, even though both areas lacked written records. In the Valley of Mexico, for example, he went to great pains to excavate the fill of the great Pyramid of the Sun in order to make seriation studies of the sherds contained therein and his field work ignored the pyramid itself. Similarly, in Peru, although there are sizable ruins of adobe walls, cities, and mounds within easy travel from Lima, and although the mountains are covered with thousands of feet of agricultural terracing, Kroeber's considerations dealt solely with ceramic styles and horizons while ignoring the other evidences of the civilization. In his university courses and in his books on civilizations he paid attention to the New World centers of culture growth and contrasted Mesoamerica and Peru by pointing out the Mesoamerican emphasis on ceremonial art, writing, and calendrical reckoning, whereas Peru was characterized by massive construction, roads, canals, and other great works. Attention to such matters, however, did not obtrude themselves in his archaeological field work which seems to have been strictly delimited by a search for diachronic sequences.

Kroeber's expanding interest in the characteristics of the early great civilizations seems almost entirely separate from the diachronic study of ceramic types and to have been stimulated by the written records of the development of civilizations, which he preferred to label "history," and for which written records of the eastern hemisphere pre-date those of the western hemisphere by several thousand years.

His interest in and courses concerning the Mesoamerican and Inca, or Andean, cultures seem to have been drawn more from contemporary Spanish sources than from archaeological reports. Excavation had not been seriously undertaken in the focal areas which contained the monumental architecture and other great achievements. These were not the subject of intensive study until after World War II. Kroeber's history of these centers in the New World, therefore, was essentially descriptive and contrastive rather than historical in the ultimate sense. Diachronic studies of the total New World civilizations, rather than simply of the ceramic horizon sequences, would have inevitably disclosed considerable parallelism of development.

John Rowe (1962, p. 408) explains an interesting reversal of the diachronic aspects of ethnology and archaeology during Kroeber's lifetime. He points out that when Kroeber began his professional work there was, with the possible exception of Max Uhle's work, "effectively no time depth in archaeology," for archaeology had been mainly concerned with classifying and describing prehistoric monuments, "usually with a view of tracing regional differences." Kroeber was interested at this point in the historical inferences drawn from the distribution of culture elements which Boas had suggested, so that ethnology rather than archaeology could hope to supply whatever time depth might be available. I should add here that distribution studies had been made during the 1920s and into the 1930s, including Kroeber's element list surveys, and were the main subject matter of many doctoral theses. Rowe goes on to say that "by the time of Kroeber's death relationships of archaeology and ethnology to time had been substantially reversed. Archaeology had become overwhelmingly diachronic while ethnology was becoming timeless, increasingly concerned with the study of synchronic patterns rather than with how cultures got to be the way they are. The diachronic interest in ethnology has been largely restricted to the specialized fields of accultura-

42

tion and applied anthropology," fields which never particularly interested Kroeber partly because they did not provide data on history as Kroeber understood it. By this time the British anthropologists, especially, had attacked the age-area method because it provided very inaccurate history, and at best illuminated little more than a history of individual elements rather than elements as seen in a context of patterns or whole cultures. As Kroeber developed the diachronic aspects of archaeology he nonetheless was led to consideration of parallels, which he mentions but from which he rarely drew conclusions.

Kroeber both wrote about and taught archaeology as a diachronic subject but prior to his death, as Rowe points out, only one dissertation of thirty-four dealt with archaeology, the remainder dealing basically with comparative ethnographic data which were obtained as often from library sources as from the field. In the case of my own dissertation on the "Ceremonial Buffoon of the American Indians" (Michigan Academy of Sciences, *Arts & Letters*, XIV: 1930), Kroeber approved of the distribution studies of certain elements in the clown complex but was strongly opposed, although Lowie supported me, to my inferences concerning parallel developments, for fundamentally psychological reasons, of certain themes of humor which in fact were world wide in occurrence.

ELEMENT LIST SURVEY

During the early decades of American anthropology the plotting of element distributions and inferences made therefrom concerning their history were common. British criticism of the historical aspects of American anthropology was based on doubts concerning the age-area inferences as well as the Britons' own preoccupation with the living tribes of the British Empire. Despite Kroeber's insistence that cultures be viewed as wholes, rather than dissected into constituent elements, each treated separately, he and his students devoted a great deal of attention to plotting element distributions and inferring the history of each on the assumption that those with the widest distribution had, other things being equal, greater antiquity. Just what constituted a culture element or an irreducible component of culture was never made clear. Kroeber employed this method in his *Hand-*

book of the Indians of California. His treatment of religious manifestations assumed that shamanism, which was found everywhere, was the most ancient ingredient of religion in California, whereas religious cults found only in limited portions of the area were more recent. For example, the Kuksu cult of north central California and the initiatory ceremonies of the southern coast were judged to be the latest developments. During the late twenties many student dissertations dealt with the distributions of particular elements or element complexes; for example, W. D. Strong (An Analysis of Southwestern Society, *American Anthropologist,* XXIX, 1–61) postulated the derivation of the socio-ceremonial complex of the Indians of southern California from the Pueblo Indians on the basis of distributions that were continuous from one area to the other except as they were interrupted by the Yuman-speaking tribes of the lower Colorado River.

Use of elements and their distributions can be observed in Kroeber's inferences concerning the origins of Eskimo culture, when he uses element counts of different aspects of Eskimo culture to test opposing theories.

Finally, the same fundamental approach was used in his Huxley lecture of 1946 entitled "The Oikoumene," which was a contrast of the cultural achievements of the eastern and western hemispheres based on lists of the culture elements peculiar to each.

It might be noted parenthetically that Leslie Spier, who took his Ph.D. under Boas, had reconstructed the history of the Plains Indians sun dance on the basis of culture element distributions, but he subsequently repudiated his dissertation, about 1930, and the value of age-area distributions.

Although Kroeber's main interest in cultural studies centered in their qualitative characterization, he was drawn into quantification in the case of the Element List Survey which involved a large project carried out in the mid-thirties. Kroeber had not been indifferent to possible mathematical methods previously, and indeed his collection of readings for introductory anthropology courses included E. B. Tylor's classical work on the mother-in-law taboo. In this work Tylor had shown on simple statistical graphs that the mother-in-law taboo occurred much more frequently in cases of matrilocal residence than it did in other forms of post-marital residence. Kroeber always questioned the explanatory validity of such correlations on the grounds that diffusion of traits that were not necessarily related might bring a high correlation in their occurrence.

In the mid-twenties, while Kroeber was working over the Uhle collection, he and his students, who became co-authors, attempted to use a statistical method on the types of pots obtained from burial lots under the guidance of an expert actuary. The kind of statistical approach attempted did not pay off, however, and was abandoned. Kroeber had used a simple statistical technique, in 1915, when he did field work among the Zuñi and undertook to date the relative age of different sites in the area by simple counting of the proportion of different kinds of sherds.

An enormous amount of effort was put into the Element List Survey by a dozen or so persons working in the field. This came about, as I recollect, because the late Stanislaw Klimek, a Pole who was later killed in World War II, had heard that Kroeber was interested in statistics. The statistics in question, as I understood the development of the idea, were those of Forrest Clements, a Kroeber student with a minor in psychology, whose dissertation concerned the percentage of color blindness among Indians. Klimek arrived in Berkeley with a statistical formula which had been designed originally for treating biological data. But when applied to cultural data, it had the unique quality and presumably the advantage that it took into account the mutual absences of culture elements as well as their presences between any two cultural groups. The resulting index of similarities between these cultural groups was presented on a scale from 0 to 1, and required an enormous amount of work in each case to compute.

Kroeber obtained sufficient funds to have virtually every so-called tribe, or sociocultural group, from the Rocky Mountains to the Pacific Coast studied. Since mutual absences of culture elements presumably were significant, the members of the project began comparing lists, vying with one another to think of elements not previously included. Presences and absences were checked off in the list by simple pluses and minuses with occasional footnotes that were more fully explanatory of the item in question. The element list finally included such minutiae as means of depilation of the beard, of brushing the teeth, and indeed anything one might think of. I obtained two sets of about twenty lists each from the Numic division of the Great Basin Shoshoneans. Despite the stark simplicity of these societies, as in the case of the Gosiute Shoshoni, who perhaps had one of the simplest cultures known ethnographically in the world, the total list could amount to some 3,000 items. The element lists were all eventually published but I am not aware that any important use was ever made of them. In my own case I found this method of presenting information wholly unsuited for an account of the structure of the social groups and of the cultural ecological adaptation involved, for which reason that portion of my field work was subsequently presented in a Bureau of American Ethnology Bulletin.

Despite Klimek's early assertions that this was the only "correct way" to do culture history, Kroeber apparently felt after a few years that he had entered a blind alley and abandoned interest in the project. Harold Driver was most persistent in pursuing the method, and the culture element distributions thus obtained became basic to his book on the American Indian.

Dealing with culture elements and their distributions was not new in American ethnology. Wissler and many others, including even Boas, had done so previously but the element list survey marked the culmination of attempts to dissect culture into units which could be approached distributionally, which, in fact, always seemed to me to violate Kroeber's own basic point of view.

In viewing Kroeber's place in the history of anthropology, especially now that so much attention is given to the so-called new methods of the New Anthropology, it is important to remember that he had made important contributions in his various efforts and that he was always eager to explore any new possibilities. In this case the effort happened not to lead anywhere.

CULTURAL EVOLUTION

Kroeber's attitudes toward history are self consistent and defensible provided one is interested in the contrastive views he takes. If, in a relativistic vein, he stresses the distinguishing characteristics of cultures, no one can find fault with his views though one may wish to emphasize also those regularities which cross cultures and lead potentially to more explanatory hypotheses. On the question of cultural evolution, however, I find Kroeber's basic assumptions and deductions therefrom inconsistent and incomprehensible; for the similarities that Kroeber sees between biological taxonomy and its basis for biological evolution, and cultural taxonomy and its relationship to cultural evolution seem to be untenable.

I was unaware that Kroeber had discussed evolution at length with Sir Julian Huxley and Père Teilhard until I read of this in Theodora Kroeber's biography. Kroeber's participation in the centennial celebration of Darwin's *Origin of Species* in Chicago in 1959 came as something of a surprise, for I had assumed that Kroeber was indifferent to the subject. However, the Darwin Centennial was celebrated widely throughout the nation and I have described it elsewhere. My contacts with and knowledge of Sir Julian Huxley were limited largely to a few admonitory letters from him pointing out that cultural evolution was merely an extension of biological evolution, a point which in its general meaning did not seem to require argument but which lacked specificity. I still do not know precisely what Huxley and Père Teilhard contributed to Kroeber's thinking on the subject of cultural evolution, although I feel that this is the one major point in Kroeber's scholarly thinking in which he seriously erred.

Kroeber believed that the principal task of "natural history"—he only occasionally called it "natural science"—was classification; for any museum must classify its collections, whether for storage or display, in such categories as function, provenience, or style. He justified this aspect of anthropology by reference to the role of taxonomy developed prior to Darwin by Linnaeus and Couvier in the biological sciences. He stressed the crucial importance of these taxonomies to the diachronic or developmental evolutionary theory of Darwin.

Cultural taxonomies as conceived by Kroeber were very different from biological ones. Uncertainty concerning criteria of cultural categories has lingered in anthropology to the present time, and many so-called cultural evolutionists continue to be trapped by the confusion caused by attempting to see cultural taxonomies as analogous to biology.

The criteria of biological classification which permitted their arrangement in an evolutionary scheme were homologies of structure. A whale or seal, for example, is classed as a mammal rather than a fish because it has lungs for breathing air, gives birth to living offspring which it nurses with mammary glands, and even its flippers morphologically, bone by bone, correspond to the legs of land mammals. By such biological taxonomy life forms are grouped in categories of increasing magnitude in varieties, species, genera, families, and so on to phyla.

Kroeber was, of course, fully aware of the distinction between analogies and homologies as he discussed it at length in his article for the Darwin Centennial but the significance of this distinction seems to have disappeared in his construction of cultural taxonomies and their place in cultural evolution. Cultural evolution was, of course, made possible by the biological evolution of man's brain and other physical features but it could not be interpreted according to the same principles as biological evolution.

Kroeber was in complete accord with Leslie White's concept of the "culturological," which was used in a sense identical with his superorganic, but he disagreed sharply with White's further understanding of evolution and its relationship to history, functionalism and science. It is not difficult to accept Kroeber's criticism of White's definition of history as a subject that deals with the particulars of events and episodes, but his further strictures on White's views are difficult to understand. Whereas White sees cultural evolutionism as introducing a historical dimension to kinds of conclusions reached by functionalism which he regards as science, Kroeber appears to reject this procedure on the grounds that a true science should consist of precise, quantitatively predictable formulations and that this is not true of cultural studies in which a high degree of unpredictability exists because culture consists of elements, styles, and patterns in their unique contexts, contiguities, and configurations.

If, therefore, it is conceded that no formulations of cultural phenomena can have a precise predictable value comparable to that of inorganic sciences, there remains the crucially important question of whether a formulation that falls somewhat short of such predictive potentials can be called a science. This statement is not in defense of White. Rather it is a contention that causal factors may nonetheless be assessed with high probability in the absence of one hundred percent demonstrable effects.

An evolutionist can scarcely disregard the spatial aspects of culture and the historical implications of such contiguity, and thereby the problems of diffusion as well as independent invention, but a causal formulation stating a high degree of probability may be made by taking into account those features of culture which are functionally transformed in diffusion or which demonstrably have their own unique history, diffused or not. (*Nature of Culture*, p. 950.)

Kroeber's repudiation of causality seems to rest on its dealing with particular aspects rather than the entirety of culture. There are aspects of social organization which exhibit cross-cultural similarities because they are cultural-ecological adaptations, because they are limited features of kinship terminologies, because they represent class structure, or because of other features not common to all cultures. The causality involved in each case is very convincing, though never comparable to that of the physical sciences.

Kroeber's taxonomy of cultures was in no way based on homologous structures or any other attributes comparable to biological homologies. His basis for assessing cultures may best be called style. The analogy of cultural emphasis to that of the individual did not mean any reductionism to psychology, for Kroeber was unrelentingly opposed to such reductionism. It did mean, however, that he ascribed great importance to style in the much broader sense, which tended strongly to be aesthetically tinged. He variously characterized cultures by their principal manifestations, the Maya by their achievements in writing and calendrical systems, architectural forms, and decorative art; and by contrast the Inca by their accomplishments in vast irrigation works, roads, and bridges, and their organizing ability. In fact, Kroeber's major works were devoted to classification of cultures and civilizations on the basis of distinctive styles: *Configura-*

49

tions of Culture Growth, much of *Anthropology, An Anthropologist Looks at History,* and a *Roster of Civilizations and Cultures,* the last preliminary and incomplete notes, published posthumously.

The basis of Kroeber's taxonomy was really the contrasts between cultures rather than a Linnaean-like system based on morphological homologies. If one culture was somewhat similar to another, it had been exposed to it through proximity and acquired resemblances through having shared some of the historical tradition or through diffusion. In biological forms, however, traits are genetically determined and cannot be transmitted to other species and genera, a fact Kroeber recognized but did not utilize in his views of cultural evolution. The Linnaean significance of Kroeber's natural history or classificatory efforts, therefore, is not valid. His is a cultural relativist position, and he cites with approval Benedict's *Patterns of Culture,* especially her contrast of the Dionysian and Apollonian patterns of the Plains Indians and Pueblo.

At the same time, Kroeber stressed the taxonomic analogy of culture with biology, seeing the main task of anthropology as recognition of the patterns—i.e., styles—of culture, "which in principle at least might be classifiable. The anthropologists have most consistently examined sociocultural units as they seem to occur more or less segregated in nature and history." (1962, p. 14.) Kroeber advocates further attention both to the small cultures, or those of tribal societies, and to the great civilizations of history as a means of "viewing them in their interrelations, both as to the spread and interflow of their content, and as to their adjacencies and similarities and groupings." (1962, p. 15.) The grouping of cultures in culture areas, he states, provided "classifications . . . somewhat comparable to the pre-Darwinian taxonomies of the plant and animal kingdoms; and like them they contained an implicit developmental history." "I regard such formulations as one of the things that the world of learning has the right to expect from anthropology." (1962, pp. 15–16.)

Kroeber's *Roster of Civilizations and Cultures* (1962) is little more than preliminary notes for a classification or "natural history of the world's cultures, living and extinct." It suggests both temporally and territorially delimited cultures and subcultures. As in his doctoral dissertation (1901) on Arapaho art, he regarded culture as consisting of many interrelated tendencies that are "both eternally living and everlastingly changing. They flow into one another; they transform themselves; they are indistinguishably combined where they coexist."

If Kroeber regarded the need for classification as basic to natural history, his basis for classification was anything but natural history. Instead of comparable morphological features, he always looked for stylistic features, which was extended to mean the emphasis that characterized and distinguished each culture. His apparent desire to reconstruct world cultures throughout history as a tree-like form, which he himself repudiated, comparable to the evolutionary interpretation of biological taxonomies, was impossible; for cultural patterns or forms that have diverged may, unlike biological taxa above the specific level, cross over and blend with one another. Kroeber could not therefore have postulated any cultural evolutionary scheme. And he could not deal with causality; for his emphasis on style meant attention to cultural achievements of dissimilar orders. In addition to contrasts such as those between the Mayan and Inca cultures, he contrasted the ascetic philosophy of India with the sense of political loyalty of Japan. Similar contrasts are set forth in his *Configurations of Culture Growth* and *An Anthropologist Looks at History*. His life was devoted to an understanding of the nature of culture, in which style or emphasis loomed as all important, though increasing attention was paid to the values implicit in each culture.

It is significant that Kroeber rarely wrote about the nature of subsistence, economics, or political and social structure, let alone their effects on other aspects of culture. That the dissimilar achievements of the Maya and the Inca were both built on dense, stable agricultural populations controlled by state structures was to Kroeber a matter for the social scientist, whom he distrusted.

Kroeber's classification therefore could lead to no system based on comparability. To the contrary, any characterization of a culture was significant because it stressed differences. This was partly an argument against a genetic basis for the distinctiveness of any culture, partly an avoidance of social science. Social science, he felt, dealt excessively with practical problems, and set up hypotheses that too commonly used statistical methods. And yet, he often marshaled his data in such a way as to beg causal interpretation which he was unwilling to give.

CAUSALITY

Kroeber always seriously doubted the possibility of making causal explanations of cultural phenomena, but in several essays it seems to me he came close to doing so, although he always stopped short of a final causal explanation.

In a paper dealing with changes in burial customs in the southwest he deliberately set himself the problem of whether the nature of the disposal of the dead resisted change owing to the extent to which it was presumably emotion laden. He noted that a shift from burial to cremation or other modes of disposing of the dead was apparently not affected in the least by the emotion involved. This gave a negative answer to the question of causality.

In a paper that dealt with Australia and relied heavily upon Radcliffe-Brown's data,[3] Kroeber concluded that the residential and subsistence groups were the most stable whereas the marriage classes, moieties, and other divisions were "embroideries upon the basic fabric." This conclusion concerning the comparative stability of social features came very near to a postulate of causality of social relations to environment and subsistence factors, although he did not quite say so.

In the 1948 edition of his *Anthropology*, Kroeber devoted a few pages to reviewing the developmental similarities between the early civilizations of the Old and New Worlds. These similarities were so great as seemingly to beg explanation but, after pointing them out, Kroeber went no further in drawing causal inferences.

In dealing with the more circumscribed phenomena of the changes in women's dress styles, as indicated mainly by the length of the skirt, he postulated tentatively that the more drastic changes tended

[3] 1938. "Basic and Secondary Patterns of Social Structure," *Journal Royal Anthropological Institute of Great Britain and Ireland*, 103A. 12 pp.

to occur during periods of social unrest. (*Anthropology* [1948], p. 334.)

This hesitancy to deal with explanations, though I believe fundamentally Kroeber's doubt of the validity of any that might be proposed, reflects his own preoccupation with style and values which are far more difficult to explain and also resulted from his extensive dealings with languages whose structural distinctiveness has no obvious explanation. In addition, Kroeber's holistic view of culture did not permit assignment of a primary, or causal, role to any one aspect of culture, whether subsistence, economics, religion, or art. Also, his consistent adherence to the concept that culture was superorganic prevented him from exploring causes of lower levels such as ecological or psychological adaptations.

When Kroeber said, "I am interested in phenomena" and frequently added "rather than in causes" he had reference to the primary need of natural history to classify its phenomena. To this end it was necessary to determine the basic characteristics upon which a classification was based. His lifelong interest in esthetic and stylistic features of a culture led him to ascribe somewhat equal importance to political attitudes, monumental architecture, or art forms. This brought about a search for those features of culture which were most characteristic. This procedure did not provide a firm basis for any causal interpretations, because there must be a consistency in the basis of the classificatory criteria selected.

CULTURE AND ENVIRONMENT

Kroeber's interest in environment did not concern the ways in which culture, especially the organization of people for subsistence activities, was influenced by the use of exploitative technologies in particular environments. Rather, it seems to me, Kroeber was initially interested in culture areas, which, like those of several scholars including especially Clark Wissler in his book *Man and Culture*, were relativistically defined in terms of their distinguishing characteristics or differences and occurred in different environmental settings. I am not aware that the concept of adaptation of the cultures, especially of the nature of social groups, to the environment were taken into ac-

53

count. In fact, this would smack of reductionism, which Kroeber, holding firmly to the idea that cultures should be dealt with on the superorganic level alone, had always opposed.

Kroeber's *Cultural and Natural Areas of North America* represented a continuation of his earlier interest in diffusion which had come initially from Boas's studies of the distribution of culture elements and which Kroeber and many of his students utilized in Ph.D. dissertations. The extent to which adjacent societies or tribes and culture areas shared different culture elements was, if possible, explained as diffusion. In addition, Kroeber's insistent willingness to do the grubby work of any monograph had led him to great detail in his culture area maps and led him at the same time to develop a subject of great interest to him, namely, native populations and their densities.

This interest in the environment and its resources and other characteristics had drawn Kroeber to Carl Sauer, a former professor of geography at the University of California.

FUNCTIONALISM

Kroeber took a very skeptical view of functionalism. In the late 1920s he invited Malinowski and Radcliffe-Brown to visit Berkeley at different times to conduct short series of seminars on their respective views of functionalism. Both of them took a rather strongly proselytizing approach but neither succeeded in making much impression. After both had left Berkeley, Kroeber and Lowie held a departmental seminar on functionalism in order to test its worth. The main subject, unfortunately, was house types and the problem was how a functionalist approach could be applied to house types. It got little beyond matters of house construction and conclusions were very obvious: that timbers were needed to hold up the roof, and an opening was necessary to serve as a doorway. I do not recall that the attempted application of functionalism extended to who occupied the house in terms of families or other groups, or the relationship of the house size to its occupants and to its uses.

In Kroeber's case, I believe that a major doubt about the value of functionalism stemmed in part from his general lack of interest in social structure as compared with other aspects of culture. Yet, it is a tribute to Kroeber's probing mind that he invited Malinowski and Radcliffe-Brown to Berkeley, and that he followed up their visits with his own seminar. In several sections of *Nature of Culture* Kroeber presents his criticism of functionalism more fully and theoretically. He questioned that any ahistorical method could explain much about culture and regarded the conclusions of Radcliffe-Brown and Malinowski as largely misplaced and illusory.

THE INDIVIDUAL AND CULTURE

The problem of the relationship of the individual to culture has been approached in various ways: genetically, psychologically, psychoanalytically, and biographically. Kroeber was by no means indifferent to this general problem and he drew conclusions from the data which he amply documented.

He never denied that a genetic factor may have had some effect upon culture but he took great pains to show that it was negligible, and almost impossible to ascertain. The hypothesis that a genetic factor accounted for cultural differences was tantamount to a form of racism which opens the doors for claims that there are racial differences which explain cultural differences. In ethnography, Kroeber pointed out again and again that historic depth of the antecedents of any known cultural patterns were insufficient to throw much light on them. Where one had access to the historic data of civilization, he pointed out in *Configurations of Culture Growth*, the clustering of geniuses who accounted for the achievements of civilization could not have been explained by genetic change for they occurred for relatively short periods and in limited areas. For example, the achievement of ancient Greece occurred within a few centuries after which Greece ceased to produce much in the way of outstanding achievement, a fact which could not be explained by the sudden appearance and disappearance of a genetic factor for genius. Rather, it had to be concluded that circumstances became favorable or unfavorable for the manifestation of genius which otherwise had to be presumed to exist while remaining latent.

By the same token, the theory that any individual or group had special aptitudes was equally without firm foundation. An example of Kroeber's reaction to such propositions occurred at the Darwin Centennial in Chicago in 1959, where it was proposed that certain groups had a genetic factor for floriculture. The dispute following this assertion so upset Kroeber that he walked out, as he said, to avoid working himself into a state of anger that might induce a heart attack.

Although Kroeber had taken psychology as a minor in college, he did not pursue the question of abstract I.Q.'s and in fact his own research paid practically no attention to aspects of physical anthropology, although he always kept well informed about developments in this field.

It was some time in the 1930s that a group in New York City, meeting in a seminar under Abram Kardiner, a practicing psychoanalyst, applied theories of psychoanalysis to the relationship of the individual and his culture. Margaret Mead played a role in the development of this approach, and Edward Sapir, though not on record with publications to this effect, had stimulated a concern with individual psychology among his students. The group, influenced by Kardiner, included many outstanding anthropologists such as Ralph Linton, Clyde Kluckhohn, Cora du Bois, and a dozen or so others, who participated in these symposia. The general thesis set forth was that the character of the individual was formulated in his first years of life, and thereafter changed very little. This is but one way of viewing the normative factors which combine to prevent culture change for it postulates a kind of inevitability in the continuation of fixed culture patterns.

Kroeber, despite having been psychoanalyzed and having become a lay analyst, basically repudiated a psychoanalytical approach to culture because he had previously set forth his principle that culture is a phenomenon of the superorganic, not influenced by lower levels of organization such as the organic or the intermediate level of the psychological. Kroeber was later to regret his strong insistence on this point but he never conceded the importance of the psychological factor to cultural studies, for all groups of mankind are presumed to have identical psychological processes, except as they are modified by cultural behavior. He utilized some concepts of psychoanalysis, such as infantilism, only in characterizing certain aspects or kinds of cultures.

Kroeber eschewed a general psychological, as contrasted with psychoanalytic, approach to culture for the same reasons. In this respect Kroeber deviated from the basic endeavors of Boas, who allegedly sought in cultural studies an understanding of the psychological nature of mankind. It has never been clear to me exactly what kind of understandings Boas really sought nor what kinds of conclusions, if any, Boas reached.

Kroeber did not reject the biographical approach to culture as inherently wrong but he used this approach as an exemplification of cultural phenomena rather than as an explanation. Outstanding individuals, whatever their inherent capacity, clearly occurred in history in clusters with reference to circumstances which favored them. Mention of such individuals, therefore, was useful as illustration or exemplification of facts about culture, but beyond this Kroeber would not go.

VALUES

One aspect of culture that acquired increasing significance as Kroeber grew older was its value system. This did not involve the question of whether values might be given a scientific foundation but rather the matter of the role that values assumed in any culture. There are, of course, no cultures which lack values, or guiding objectives, even though these consist of the simple aim of obtaining sufficient food to exist.

Kroeber, however, was less interested in this fairly universal and fundamental value than in the specific values that set one culture off from another. In a sense, the value orientation of a culture is contained in its emphasis, whether on art manifestations, religious themes, or other pervasive motifs. Kroeber was much impressed by Ruth Benedict's clarification of the difference in values between what she called the Dionysian pattern of the Great Plains Indians and the

Apollonian patterns of the Pueblo Indians. He was also impressed by Morris Opler's *Seven Themes in Apache Culture* which were manifestations of Apache values.

All of these values were relativistically unique to the culture in question. However, he undertook in a few pages in his *Anthropology* to characterize some of the values of primitive cultures as infantile, implying that the absence of these values indicated a more advanced state.

HISTORY

Perhaps the most distinctive characteristic of Kroeber was his inintense interest in history, especially in the recorded history of civilizations. His scope covered the diachronic development of all societies and ranged from the growth of primitive societies to the present day, including those great portions of culture history such as the early civilizations and recent cultures that anthropologists have almost entirely left to the classicists and sinologists. The basic problems, however, did not change. Kroeber continued to seek characterizing phenomena which posed the questions of the historical culminations and periodization of culture as well as their areal limitations and climaxes.

In the breadth of his scope, Kroeber covered the ground of Gibbon, Spengler, and Toynbee, but he repudiated as premature and a priori any analogy to the individual life cycle of growth and decay. He sought first to classify empirically, after which philosophical speculation might be in order.

Kroeber's emphasis on style necessarily entailed a holistic view of culture. In his discussion of human nature (1966, Chap. 14, written in 1955) he probes some of the potential styles in terms of the limitations of possibilities. Undetermined factors prescribe the ultimate limits of behavioral variations, but within these limits each culture has its emphasis: the Polynesians on cannibalism, the peoples of India on asceticism and hierarchical groupings in castes, and the Japanese in political loyalties.

A position of holism must assume that any aspect of culture or any kind of behavior within the limits of the human potential may have primary importance to the style. At the same time, it pre-cludes inquiry as to why this is so. For an explanation might shift from an assumption that religious beliefs were ultimate causes of the remainder of culture in one case, to art styles in another or to sub-sistence or economic factors in still others.

More importantly, this holism enabled Kroeber to avoid primary criteria of relevancy in cultural phenomena. It was historic processes that made any aspect of culture emerge as the dominant value or style. He could see India as characterized by asceticism formulated by Buddha rather than as an area of statelets and rigid caste struc-ture, and Japan as a nation of intense political loyalties rather than as one of feudal institutions. After he had participated in a con-ference on feudalism in honor of Toynbee, which had noted the striking resemblances of Japanese feudalism to that of northern Eu-rope, he was asked why this was so. Characteristically, he brushed aside the question by saying that they were not looking for causes in history.

This holism entails cultural relativism of a most extreme form. In any event, Kroeber's own writings rarely if ever gave a prominent place to analysis of socioeconomic and political patterns. Such pat-terns were potentially equally characteristic of some cultures, but seemed to have been minimized in favor of more "stylistic" ones in others.

Kroeber's emphasis on natural history was clearly at the expense of subsistence patterns, economics, social structure, and political forms. Important as these have been in sociology and recent anthro-pology, especially as they are related to political and social ideol-ogies, Kroeber rarely wrote about them as such. If economic features were important in a culture, that was the result of historical change. Kroeber was quite un-Marxian in his indifference to economic and social institutions.

His book *An Anthropologist Looks at History*, perhaps more than any other of Kroeber's writings, exemplifies his basic point of view. It does not differ fundamentally from his lifelong concept of culture but it does place it and sum it up in his most recent perspective. As the title of the book implies, his emphasis is on history, that is,

59

culture as known through history. He shifts his frame of discourse from ethnology to history, especially to written history. The point of view is the same as that expressed in previous writings, but his life-long interest in history was most prominently displayed in this book.

On several occasions during his early years, Kroeber had given a university course on the history of civilizations. In fact, in the late 1920s I took such a course from him in which he used H. G. Wells's *Outline of History* as the text. Kroeber had returned to this interest from time to time but he had not made it the focal point of his writing. In assembling the materials for *An Anthropologist Looks at History*, which he did intermittently during the 1950s, while a member of the Center for Advanced Study in the Behavioral Sciences, he finally expressed overtly and fully his attitudes toward history, wherein his vast knowledge had, in my opinion, earned him his enormous reputation.

Milton Singer, in his foreword to this book, underlines the main elements of Kroeber's thinking. He states (p. v) "that every culture is a complex and composite growth which derives most of its component elements from its own past or has borrowed them from other cultures; and two, that every culture tends to develop distinctive organization, coherent and self-consistent, which tends to absorb new elements, whether borrowed or indigenous, and to reshape them to accord with its own patttern."

The nature of Kroeber's emphasis is shown by a further quotation from Singer (p. xi): "Kroeber was, of course, aware of the adaptiveness of culture growth to environmental and other circumstances, particularly in the fields of subsistence and social and political organization." This covers a great deal of what is commonly known as culture. "He was more interested, however, in the birth of cultural creativity and development through shaping forces, cultural patterns and styles."

Kroeber differed from Boas in his love of history, which in many ways dominated his anthropological work more than the ethnology of primitive peoples. Not that Boas denied the importance of history but rather that in ethnography it is virtually impossible to obtain, although Boas began the development of an age-area method which was to dominate anthropology for many years. Kroeber's interest in history was more in the written records of the great civilizations than in early prehistory, for the latter was very little known during the early decades of Kroeber's career. He was not indifferent to the history of any era and yet his major contributions, especially during the latter half of his life, lay in the history of civilizations and the problems as he saw them pertaining thereto.

Kroeber differed from anthropologists more generally in his insistence that the superorganic was the proper level on which anthropology should operate. By this assumption he avoided any contention that organically determined, i.e., genetically determined, features were part of culture. His closest approach to consideration of innate human features was in an essay on human nature, written in 1958 and published in 1966, but this dealt with the possible range of human behavior. Within this vast range, his great interest was to determine the primary characteristics of each culture.

PART III

Selected Writings

This part is devoted entirely to statements of Kroeber's views from his own writings. The selection of the following passages was not easy; Kroeber's bibliography comprises some 500 titles, which in aggregate represent a tremendous diversity of subjects.

The problem was to choose from these works the statements that exemplify Kroeber's basic interests. I have been guided by views summarized in Part II. Little effort is made to group passages reproduced according to theory or subject. Samples of his writing appear in chronological order.

The Handbook of the Indians of California, which was completed in 1918 and published by the Bureau of American Ethnology in 1923, has always been a major source of California ethnology and languages. This book summarizes linguistic and ethnological research during Kroeber's first two decades in California. A small part of Yurok ethnology is reproduced.

Alfred Kroeber

The Yurok: Land and Civilization

✤ This history begins with an account of the Yurok, a nation resident on the lower Klamath River, near and along the Pacific Ocean, in extreme northern California, surrounded by peoples speaking diverse languages but following the same remarkable civilization. The complete aspect of this civilization is un-Californian. It is at bottom the southernmost manifestation of that great and distinctive culture the main elements of which are common to all the peoples of the Pacific coast from Oregon to Alaska; is heavily tinctured with locally developed concepts and institutions; and further altered by some absorption of ideas from those tribes to the south and east who constitute the true California of the ethnologist.

This civilization, which will hereafter be designated as that of northwestern California, attains on the whole to a higher level, as it is customary to estimate such averaged values, than any other that flourished in what is now the State of California. But it is better described as an unusually specialized culture, for the things in which it is deficient it lacks totally; and these are numerous and notable.

QUALITY OF CIVILIZATION

In inventions there was no marked superiority to the remainder of aboriginal California; but most arts were carried to a distinctive pitch. Manufactured articles were better finished. Many objects which the central and southern Californians fashioned only as bare utility demanded were regularly decorated with carvings in the northwest. Often the identical object was made of wood in one region and of antler or stone in the other. A new technical process is scarcely superadded by such a substitution. As regards the mere list of knowledges or faculties, the two cultures remain at par. But the northwestern preference for the more laborious material evidences a different attitude, an appreciation of values which in the ruder central and southern tracts is disregarded. That this difference is deep seated, and that it is manifest at almost every point, is evident when the slab house of the Miwok or Yuki, the canoe or maul of the Modoc, the pipe or acorn stirrer of the Pomo, the netting shuttle and spoon of the Maidu, or the obsidian blade of the Wintun, are set by the side of the corresponding utensils of the Yurok or their northwestern neighbors. It is only among the far-away Chumash that technological activities were granted a similar interest and love; and this localized southern culture has long since perished so completely as to make a comparative evaluation difficult.

The implements that are made only in the northwest—the stool, pillow, box, purse, and the like—are not very numerous. They are at least partly balanced by central and southern devices which the northwesterners lack; and they do not in any instance involve a process or mechanical faculty of which the more typical Californians are wholly ignorant.

Much the same holds of wealth. Money is prized and establishes influence everywhere in California. It certainly counts for more in private and public life among the average Californian people than among the tribes of the plains or the settled and unsettled tribes of the southwestern United States. But whatever its influence in southern or middle California, that influence is multiplied among the Yurok. Blood money, bride purchase, compensation to the year's mourners before a dance can be held, are institutions known to almost every group described in the present work. The northwesterners alone have measured the precise value of every man's life or wife or grief. Every injury, each privilege or wrong or trespass, is calculated and compensated. Without exactly adjusted payment, cessation of a feud is impossible except through utter extirpation of one party, marriage is not marriage but a public disgrace for generations, the ceremony necessary to the preservation of the order of the world is not held. The consequence is that the Yurok concerns his life above all else with property. When he has leisure, he thinks of money; if in need, he calls upon it. He schemes constantly for opportunity to lodge a claim or to evade an obligation. No resource is too mean or devious for him to essay in this pursuit.

If such endeavors are to be realized, there are needed an accurately computable scheme of economic valuation, and an elaborate and

65

precise code of rights. The northwesterner has both. His law is of the utmost refinement. A few simple and basic principles are projected into the most intricate subtleties; and there is no contingency which they do not cover. The central Californian has his law also. But it is neither rigid nor ramified. Margin is left for modification according to personality or circumstance or public opinion. There are phases of life in central California into which neither money nor legality enter.

With all this savoring so strongly of Kwakiutl and Haida custom, the Yurok is wholly Californian in his lack of any visible symbolism to give emotional expression to the economic values which are so fundamental with him. He is without crests or carvings or totems; there are no separately designated social classes, no seats in order of rank, no titles of precedence, no named and fixed privileges of priority. His society follows the aims of the societies of the North Pacific coast with the mechanism of the societies of middle California.

Property and rights pertain to the realm of the individual, and the Yurok recognizes no public claim and the existence of no community. His world is wholly an aggregation of individuals. There being no society as such, there is no social organization. Clans, exogamic groups, chiefs or governors, political units, are unrepresented even by traces in northwestern California. The germinal, nameless political community that can be traced among the Indians of the greater part of the State is absent. Government being wanting, there is no authority, and without authority there can be no chief. The men so called are individuals whose wealth, and their ability to retain and employ it, have clustered about them an aggregation of kinsmen, followers, and semidependents to whom they dispense assistance and protection. If a man usually marries outside the village in which he lives, the reason is that many of his coinhabitants normally happen to be blood relatives, not because custom or law or morality recognize the village as a unit concerned with marriage. The actual outcome among the Yurok may, in the majority of cases, be the same as among nations consciously organized on an exogamic plan. The point of view, the guiding principles both of the individual's action and of the shaping of the civilization, are wholly nonexogamic. Such familiar terms as "tribe," "village community," "chief," "government," "clan," can therefore be used with reference to the Yurok only after extreme care in previous definition—in their current senses they are wholly inapplicable.

Shamanism takes on a peculiar aspect in northwestern California in that the almost universal American Indian idea of an association between the shaman and certain spirits personally attached to him is very weakly and indirectly developed. Shamanistic power resides in control of "pains," small animate objects, nonanimal and nonhuman in shape, which on the one hand cause illness by entering the bodies of men, and on the other endow the shaman with power when he brings them to reside within himself, or rather herself, for practically all shamans are women. The witch or poisoner is usually a man and operates by magic rather than shamanistic faculty. In the remainder of California the distinction between the maker and the curer of disease is almost effaced, the shaman being considered indifferently malevolent or beneficent according to circumstances, but operating by the exercise of the same powers.

Concepts relating to magic are as abundantly developed among the Yurok and their neighbors as shamanism is narrowed. Imitative magic is particularly favored and is often of the most crudely direct kind, such as performing a simple action or saying the desired thing over and over again. The thousand and one occasions on which magic of this rather bare volitional type is employed reveal a tensity that usually seems brought on consciously. This emotional tautness, which contrasts glaringly with the slack passivity and apathetic sluggishness of the average California Indian, is manifest in other matters. Thus, restraint and self-control in manner and in relations with other men are constantly advocated and practiced by the Yurok.

Northwestern religion is colored by the cultural factors already enumerated. The idea of organization being absent, there are no cult societies or initiations. Symbolism is an almost unknown attitude of mind except in matters of outright magic: therefore masks, impersonations, altars, and sacred apparatus, as such, are not em-

67

ployed. The tangible paraphernalia of public ceremony are objects that possess a high property value—wealth that impresses, but nevertheless profane and negotiable wealth. The dances are displays of this wealth as much as they are song and step. All life being individualized instead of socialized, the ceremonies attach to specified localities, much as a fishing place and an individual's right to fish are connected. In the remainder of California, where stronger communal sense exists, the precise location of the spot of the dance becomes of little moment in comparison with the circumstances of the ceremony.

The esoteric element in northwestern dances and rites of public import has as its central feature the recitation of a formula. This is not a prayer to divinities, but a narrative, mostly in dialogue, recounting the effect of an act or a series of acts, similar to those about to be performed, by a member of an ancient, prehuman, half-spirit race. The recital of this former action and its effect is believed to produce the identical effect now. The point of view is distinctly magical. Similar formulas are used for the most personal purposes: luck in the hunt, curing of sickness, success in love, the accumulation of wealth. These formulas are private property; those spoken at public ceremonials are no exception: their possessor must be paid, though he operates for the good of all.

Yurok mythology is woven in equally strange colors. Stirring plot is slighted; so are the suspense of narrative, the tension of a dramatic situation—all the directly human elements which, however rude their development, are vividly present in the traditions of most of the Californians and many other divisions of American Indians. A lyric, almost elegiac emotion suffuses the northwestern myths and tales. Affection, homesickness, pity, love of one's natal spot, insatiable longing for wealth, grief of the prehuman people at their departure before the impending arrival of mankind, are sentiments expressed frequently and often with skill. Events and incidents are more baldly depicted, except where the effect of the action recounted is the establishment of an existing practice or institution; and in these cases the myth is often nearly indistinguishable from a magical formula. Tales that will interest a child or please a naïve

68

stranger of another civilization do not appeal to the Yurok, who have developed refinedly special tastes in nearly everything with which they concern themselves.

Kroeber's Anthropology, *which was first published in 1923 as an introductory text, was the only one available at that time. Over the years,* Anthropology *was expanded, revised, and finally republished in 1948. By then it had become a compendium of most of Kroeber's theoretical and substantive writings. The selection chosen here deals with language, one of Kroeber's vital interests.*

Language

LINGUISTIC RELATIONSHIP: THE SPEECH FAMILY

✠ The question that the historian and the anthropologist most frequently ask of the philologist is whether this and that language are not related. Relationship in such connection means descent from a common source, as two brothers are descended from the same father, or two cousins from a common grandfather. If languages can be demonstrated to possess such common source, it is clear that the peoples who spoke them must at one time have been in close contact, or perhaps have constituted a single people. If, on the other hand, the languages of two peoples prove wholly dissimilar, though their racial types and cultures be virtually identical, as indeed is sometimes found to be the case—witness the Hungarians and their neighbors—it is evident that an element of discontinuous development must somewhere be reckoned with. Perhaps one part of an originally single racial group gradually modified its speech beyond recognition; or under the shock of conquest, migration, or other historical accident it may have entirely discarded its language in favor of a new and foreign tongue.

Or the opposite may be true: The two groups were originally wholly separate and distinct in many respects, but, being brought into contact, their cultures interpenetrated, intermarriage followed, and the two physical types became assimilated into one while the languages remained dissimilar. In short, if one wishes full understanding of a people, one must take its language into consideration. This means that the language must be classified. If a classification is to be more than merely logical or theoretical, if it is to be pragmatic and historically significant, it must have reference to relationship, development, origin. In a word, it must be a genetic classification.

The term used to indicate that two or more languages have a common source but are unrelated to certain others, or seem so in the present state of knowledge, is "linguistic family." "Linguistic stock" is frequently used as a synonym. This is the fundamental concept in the historical classification of languages. Without a clear idea of its meaning one involves oneself in confusion on attempting to use philology as an aid to other branches of human history.

There is no abstract reason against referring to a group of unrelated languages as a "family" because they are all spoken in one area, nor against denominating as "families," as has sometimes been done, the major subdivisions of a group of languages admittedly of common origin. Again, languages that show certain similarities of type or structure, such as inflection, might conceivably be put into one "family." But there is this objection to all such usages: They do not commit themselves on the point of genetic relationship, or they contradict it, or only partially exhaust it. Yet commonness of origin is so important in many connections that it is indispensable to have one term that denotes its ascertainable presence. And for this quality there happens to be no generally understood designation other than "linguistic family," or its synonym, "linguistic stock." This phrase will therefore be used here strictly in the sense of the whole of a group of languages sprung from a single source, and only in that sense. Other groupings will be indicated by phrases like "languages of such and such an area," "subfamily," "division of a family," or "unrelated languages of similar type."

CRITERIA OF RELATIONSHIP

The question that first arises in regard to linguistic families is how the relationship of their constituent idioms is determined. In brief, the method is one of comparison. If a considerable proportion of the words and the grammatical forms of two languages are reasonably similar, similiar enough to indicate that the resemblances cannot be due to mere accident, these similar words and forms must go back to a common source; and if this source is not borrowing by one language from another, the two tongues are related by descent from a common ancestor. If comparison fails to bring out any such degree of resemblance, the languages are classed in distinct families.

Of course it is possible that the reason two languages seem unrelated is not that they are really so, but that they have in the lapse of ages become so much differentiated that one cannot any longer find resemblance between their forms. In that event true relationship would be obscured by remoteness. Theoretically, there is high probability that many families of languages customarily regarded as totally distinct do go back in the far past to a common origin, and that our ignorance of their history, or inability to analyze them deeply, prevents recognition of their relationship. From time to time it happens that groups of languages which at first seemed unrelated are shown by more intensive study to possess elements enough in common to compel the recognition of their original unity. In that case what were supposed to be several "families" become merged in one. The scope of a particular family may be thus enlarged; but the scope of the generic concept of "family" is not altered.

Whether there is any hope that comparative philology may ultimately be prosecuted with sufficient success to lead all the varied forms of human speech back to a single origin is an interesting speculation. A fair statement is that such a possibility, like any future event, cannot be absolutely denied, but that science is still extremely far from such a realization. Of more immediate concern is an ordering and summarizing of the knowledge in hand with a view to such positive inferences as can be drawn.

71

In an estimate of the similarity of languages, items that count as evidence must meet two requirements: they must be alike, or traceably similar, or regularly correspondent in sound; and they must be alike or similar or related in meaning. This double requirement holds equally whether full words or separable parts of words, roots, or grammatical forms are compared. The English word *eel* and the French *île*, meaning *island*, are pronounced almost exactly alike, yet their meaning is so different that no sane person would regard them as sprung from the same origin. As a matter of fact *île* is derived from Latin *insula*, and is the source of the English *isle*, whereas *eel* has a cognate in German *aal*. These prototypes *insula* and *aal* being as different in sound as they are in meaning, any possibility that *eel* and *île* might be related is easily disposed of. Yet if the Latin and German cognates were lost, if nothing were known of the history of the English and French languages, and if *île* meant not *island* but, say, *fish* or *water snake*, then it might be reasonable to think of a connection.

Such doubtful cases, of which a certain proportion are likely to be adjudged wrongly, are bound to come up in regard to the less well investigated languages, particularly those of nations without writing, the earlier stages of whose speech have perished without trace. In proportion as more is known of the history of a language, or as careful analysis can reconstruct more of its past stages, the number of such border-line cases obviously becomes fewer.

Before genetic connection between two languages can be thought of, the number of their elements similar in sound and sense must be reasonably large. An isolated handful of resemblances obviously are either importations—loan words—or the result of coincidence. Thus in the native Californian language known as Yuki, *ko* means *go*, and *kom* means *come*. Yet examination of Yuki reveals no further similarities. It would therefore be absurd to dream of a connection: one swallow does not make a summer. This lone pair of resemblances means nothing except that the mathematical law of probability has operated. Among the thousands of words in one language, a number are likely to be similar in sound to words of another language; and of this number again a small fraction, perhaps one or two or five in all, will happen to bear some resemblance in meaning also. In short, the similarities upon which a verdict of genetic relationship is based must be sufficiently numerous to fall well beyond the possibility of mere coincidence; and it must also be possible to prove with reasonable certainty that they are not the result of one language's borrowing words from another, as, for instance, English has borrowed from French and Latin.

At the same time it is not necessary that the similarities extend to the point of identity. In fact, too close a resemblance between part of the stock of two languages immediately raises a presumption of borrowing. For every language is continually changing, and once a mother tongue has split into several daughters, each of these goes on modifying its sounds, and gradually shifting the meaning of its words, generation after generation. In short, where connection is real, it must be veiled by a certain degree of change or distortion.

Take the English word *foot* and the Latin word of the same meaning, *pes*. To offhand inspection the sounds or forms of the two words do not seem similar. The resemblance becomes more definite in other forms of *pes*, for instance the genitive case *ped-is* or the accusative *ped-em*. Obviously the stem or elementary portion of the Latin word is not *pes* but *ped-*; and the *d* is closer to the English *t* of *foot* than is the *s* of *pes*. The probability of relationship is increased by the Greek word for foot, *pous*, whose stem proves to be *pod-*, with vowel closer to that of English. Meanwhile, it would be recognized that there are English words beginning with *ped-*, such as *pedal, pedestrian, pedestal*, all of which have a clear association with the idea of foot. All these words however possess almost exact equivalents in Latin. One would therefore be justified in concluding from these facts what indeed the history of the languages proves: namely, that *pedal, pedestrian*, and *pedestal* are Latin words taken over into English; whereas *foot* and *pes* and *pous*, and for that matter German *fuss*, are derivatives from a common form that once existed in the now extinct mother tongue from which Greek and Latin and English and German are derived.

73

Chronologically, the next work was Cultural and Natural Areas of Native North America (1939) *which deals, in large measure, with the spatial difference and separation of cultures rather than the time differences, and is based on New World material.*

Cultural and Natural Areas of Native North America

I. OBJECTIVES

✤ This study has two objectives. It aims, first, to review the environmental relations of the native cultures of North America. Its second purpose is to examine the historic relations of the culture areas, or geographical units of cultures.

Three points are best stated explicitly at the outset, to prevent possible misconception.

The first is that the present work in no sense represents a relapse toward the old environmentalism which believed it could find the causes of culture in environment. While it is true that cultures are rooted in nature, and can therefore never be completely understood except with reference to that piece of nature in which they occur, they are no more produced by that nature than a plant is produced or caused by the soil in which it is rooted. The immediate causes of cultural phenomena are other cultural phenomena. At any rate, no anthropologist can assume anything else as his specific working basis. But this does not prevent the recognition of relations between nature and culture, nor the importance of these relations to the full understanding of culture.

The second point is to guard against the possible misconception that the determination of culture areas is here considered an end in itself. The concept of a culture area is a means to an end. The end may be the understanding of culture processes as such, or of the historic events of culture.

The study of processes tends to be analytic, and therefore to dis-

* ORIGINALLY PUBLISHED by the University of California Press; reprinted by permission of The Regents of the University of California.

regard time and space relations except so far as they condition the particular phenomena whose processes are being examined. In proportion as the study advances and learns to deal more directly with cultural processes as such, the time and space relations become a sort of frame. They remain factors that for scientific purposes must be controlled, but this control becomes a limitation, almost an encumbrance. This type of study is akin to the dissecting technique of the laboratory, even though cultural anthropology has neither laboratory nor experiment. It is the method which has been carried farthest, in penetration and exactness, by Franz Boas. This method can use culture areas only to a limited extent, as a sort of preliminary; and its practitioners therefore esteem the concept as of only incidental utility.

On the contrary, the historic approach, remaining concerned with events as they occur in nature, always stresses the time aspects of phenomena as part of its ultimate objective. Ethnology, particularly when concerned with peoples which, like the native ones of America, have left few or no documentary records, perforce has recourse to spatial classifications such as culture areas. In themselves these yield only a momentary and static organization of knowledge, whereas the purpose of history is genetic. In proportion as the recognition of culture areas becomes an end in itself, it therefore defeats really historic understanding. The conception on which the present monograph is based is that space and time factors are sufficiently interrelated in culture history to make the culture area a valuable mechanism, rather than a distraction, in the penetration of the time perspective of the growth of cultures so relatively undocumented as are those of native America.

The third point to be kept in mind is that the present study deals with culture wholes, and not, except incidentally, with culture elements or "traits," nor with those associations of elements which are sometimes called "culture complexes" but which always constitute only a fraction of the entirety of any one culture. Culture wholes as a concept correspond in many ways to regional floras and faunas, which are accumulations of species but can also be viewed as summation entities.

The term "culture area" is employed because usage has established it. It is an unfortunate designation in that it puts emphasis on the area, whereas it is usually the cultural content that is being primarily considered. We mean a regionally individualized type or specific growth of culture when we say "culture area," much as a historian may use "the Eighteenth Century" as a short way of referring to the culture that was characteristic of eighteenth-century Europe. It would be well if there were a brief technical term for the naturally individualized growth of culture with which historical anthropology is more and more dealing. But it seems impossible to find an unambiguous term without coining it.[1] Evidently the general thought of our day is not yet sufficiently concerned with such growths of culture to feel the need of a designation for them.

II. HISTORY OF CONCEPTS

Environment in anthropology. For a generation American anthropologists have given less and less attention to environmental factors. In part this represents a healthy reaction against the older naïve view that culture could be "explained" or derived from the environment. For the rest, it is the result of a sharpening of specific anthropological method and the consequent clearer perception of culture forms, patterns, and processes as such: the recognition of the importance of diffusion, for instance, and of the nature of the association of culture elements into "complexes." Most attention came to be paid, accordingly, to those parts of culture which readily show self-sufficient forms: ceremonial, social organization, art, mythology; somewhat less to technology and material culture; still less to economics and politics, and problems of subsistence. Much of the anthropology practiced in this country in the present century has been virtually a sociology of native American culture; strictly historic and geographic interests have receded into the background, except where archaeological preoccupation kept them alive. We have had intensive studies of the

---

[1] "Diaita" (Angl. diaeta) has been suggested to me by J. L. Myres as an etymologically adequate term to denote a culture whole or actually cohering culture mass, corresponding to the "biota" of biologists. It would be useful if adopted.

internal social grouping of peoples of whom we did not know whether they constituted one or several national units; analyses of the patterns of maize- or acorn-utilization complexes, rather than consideration of whether such a complex provided a tenth, a half, or four-fifths of the subsistence of the various tribes who adhered to it; and so on. This diversion of attention to cultural forms was necessary and desirable; the attendant shift of interest away from historical and subsistence problems was probably inevitable. There is also often a readier productivity in work along the formal lines, especially among Indians on reservations. An old informant can sometimes give exact data on the sequence of details of a ritual that has been abandoned for forty years, but is vague about the proportion of acorns or salmon in his father's diet, or the months of each year spent by his group on the river or in the mountains. However, such facts are also of consequence in their relation to culture, since every culture is conditioned by its subsistence basis. The culminations of culture obviously rest on a certain degree of economic surplus, for instance. Such a surplus will not explain why the lines in a given art are curved instead of straight, or why a people derives the origin of mankind from below ground rather than from the sky. But it may help to explain why Haida art is esthetically richer than Kwakiutl, or Pueblo ritual more complex than Havasupai. And these are also legitimate problems; and strictly historical ones. We need not edge away from them because they involve qualitative judgments or a concern with culture wholes. Anthropology does not have to be exclusively analytic in order to be valid.

Culture Areas, Climaxes, and Boundaries. The concept of the culture area has had a gradual, empirical, almost unconscious growth. It probably began, as Boas points out, with the classification of museum collections on natural geographical lines instead of evolutionistically schematic ones. By 1916, Sapir in his Time Perspective discussed culture areas as something in general use; in 1917, Wissler codified those of native America,—on the basis, largely, of current usage. There have been no serious modifications or criticisms of his scheme. But it is significant that Wissler does not develop his interpretation of the

77

growth of American culture through use of the culture areas which he defines. He follows agriculture, the textile arts, architecture, and so on, one by one through the two continents; and it is the summation of these findings, essentially, that yields his picture of hemispheric history. The culture-area classification remains a nearly static one, and apart.

There has been another method of geographical attack: consideration of the distribution of single culture elements or limited complexes. This is the method pursued with such eminent success by Nordenskiöld in South America. Nothing equally systematic has been attempted for North America. But on a more limited scale the method has been applied by the Danes to Eskimo culture, by Spier to the Havasupai and their neighbors, and by several students to mythological material, although these latter have applied it without primarily historical objective. Wissler has used the method abundantly in somewhat different form: for larger complexes, or for summary outlines, or in elaboration of the age-and-area principle. This method is analytic in the sense that it deals with detached parts of culture. But cultures occur in nature as wholes; and these wholes can never be entirely formulated through consideration of their elements. The culture-area concept does attempt to deal with such culture wholes.

Boas has attempted to limit the significance of culture areas by asserting that these areas do not coincide when they are formulated on the basis of different parts of culture: technology, social organization, ritual, art, music, myth, etc. This view must be doubted as contrary to the overwhelming run of the facts, though no doubt occasionally true. An unusually rich development in almost all these lines is normally found coincident in highly specialized and distinctive cultures, such as those of the Pueblos or North Pacific Coast Indians.[1]

---

[1] Negative developments in relatively rich cultures are an apparent exception which really confirms the situation depicted, because absences tend to be due to strong positive developments in allied directions: the shaman is lacking in Pueblo life because the priesthood is strong, Lower Colorado tribes use a minimum of ritual paraphernalia because of their extreme emphasis on dream experience, and so on.

Navaho altar paintings may be the most developed in the Southwest, but Navaho culture is after all close to that of the Pueblos and in many ways obviously dependent on it. That at some points the pupil departs from the master or surpasses him does not invalidate the reality of a school or tradition. In general, the experience of Old World history is to the same effect.

As a matter of fact, the points in time and space at which historically known culture growths culminated usually show a virtual coincidence of florescence in the several facets of culture: the peaks of empire, wealth, sculpture, drama, philosophy, science in fifth-century Athens, for instance. Augustan Rome is another classical example; so is sixteenth-century Spain. Among other scholars, Flinders Petrie has gone so far as to try to demonstrate a fixed order in which the respective peaks of each of these facets of culture are reached in any civilizational culmination.[2] This attempt must be regarded as somewhat forced into a scheme. But it does show clearly the correlation of the parts, their close relation or overlapping coincidence in time and space, whenever the culmination is strong. There is no reason to believe that the course of events was materially different in native America. For the Maya and Pueblos we have archaeological justification that it was similar.

The whole subject of cultural climax is evidently related to that of the culture area. Since ethnologists normally deal with relatively timeless data they have been cautious and slow to approach problems of time climax. They have, however, evolved a spatial substitute: the culture center, or district of greatest cultural productivity and richness. This obviously is the regional expression of a culmination whose temporal manifestation is the climax. As so often, Wissler has pioneered the way. He makes the point that the center is the integral thing about an area. The area may therefore be conceived and represented somewhat diagrammatically. Hence the straight lines and sharp angles on Wissler's culture-classification maps. No serious exception could be taken to these maps if the centers were decisively defined; but Wissler more often than not leaves them as indefinite as the

[2] Discussed further in the final section of the present work.

area. His Plains group comprises thirty-three tribes, of which eleven are the most typical; his Southeast centers among the Muskogians, Yuchi, and Cherokee, who occupied half of the total region. For the Mackenzie and Eastern Woodland areas, the localization of centers is attempted very half-heartedly. Wissler also makes but little more use of his culture centers than of his culture areas when he reconstructs the outline history of the hemisphere. In short, it is clear that he has perceived the significance of focal points of growth, resulting in culminations definable in spatial and presumably temporal terms; but his working out of these has remained summary and indefinite.

The weakest feature of any mapping of culture wholes is also the most conspicuous: the boundaries.[3] Where the influences from two culture climaxes or foci meet in equal strength is where a line must be drawn, if boundaries are to be indicated at all. Yet it is just there that differences often are slight. Two peoples classed as in separate areas yet adjoining each other along the interarea boundary almost inevitably have much in common. It is probable that they normally have more traits in common with each other than with the peoples at the focal points of their respective areas. This is almost certain to be so where the distance from the foci is great and the boundary is not accentuated by any strong physical barrier or abrupt natural change. But the same holds true of the faunal and floral areas used by naturalists. In short, what boundaries really show is not so much clefts occurring in nature, as relative extent and strength of influences emanating from foci. They represent something comparable to political spheres of influence expressed by devices suitable for showing artificial political entities. It would be desirable, therefore, to construct cultural maps without boundary lines, on some system of shading or tint variation of color; but the mechanical difficulties are great. For the present, it seems necessary to use the old devices and leave it to the reader to translate what his eye sees into the dynamic aspects that are intended. This difficulty inheres in all attempts to

---

[3] This is less true of complexes or associations than of wholes, and is not at all applicable to atomic culture elements which can be mapped in terms of presence or absence.

express in static two-dimensional space terms, phenomena that have a sequential as well as a spatial aspect; a flow as well as a distribution.

Relation of Natural to Cultural Areas. We can accept Wissler's findings on the relation of culture areas to environment.[4] He concludes that environment does not produce a culture, but stabilizes it. Because at many points the culture must be adapted to the environment, the latter tends to hold it fast. Cultures therefore incline to change slowly once they have fitted themselves to a setting, and to enter a new environment with more difficulty than to spread over the whole of the natural area in which their form was worked out. If they do enter a new type of territory, they are subject to change. Once fitted to an environment, they are likely to alter radically only through some factor profoundly affecting subsistence, such as the introduction of agriculture.

Beyond these sound general principles, however, Wissler does not go very far. In his *American Indian* he enumerates some suggestive rough correspondences between altitude contours and linguistic or culture groups.[5] His later work, *The Relation of Nature to Man in Aboriginal North America* (1926), is concerned with the spatial distribution of culture traits and complexes. Nature in the sense of the varying physical and organic environment does not really enter into the argument, except in the last section of the last chapter, which points out, with a few examples, that ecological factors may be of importance, but does not pursue the subject to any intensive conclusions.

Wissler's ten North American culture areas really rest on the six "food" areas which he reviews at the beginning of his book on the American Indian, although the relation of the two classifications is not wholly exact and does not become very explicit. These subsistence areas seem to refer primarily to the basis of culture, but of course involve environment also, especially its ecological aspects.

Some years before, Otis T. Mason had dealt directly though summarily with the environment of cultures, in the *Handbook of American Indians.* His twelve "ethnic environments" are defined in both

[4] The *American Indian* (1922 ed.), 372–374.   [5] The same, 368–369.

geographical and cultural terms; and the environments are largely faunal and floral, that is, ecological. This stimulating essay has attracted little attention, in spite of its obvious soundness.

Configurations of Culture Growth, *published in 1944, was distinctive in that it deals sequentially with the development of culture with emphasis on culture of civilized societies of the eastern hemisphere. Space permits reproduction from this volume of only the theoretically most important portions, the Preface, Problem and Procedure, and the Conclusions. This book largely complements* Cultural and Natural Areas of Native North America.

Preface

✤ One of the recognized characteristics of human culture is the tendency of its successes or highest values to occur close together in relatively brief periods within nations or limited areas. While reasons have been adduced for the phenomenon, no systematic examination of the facts seems ever to have been made. I present here the more readily datable facts—for time lapse seems an essential factor of the phenomenon—in an orderly arrangement, as basis for an inductive comparison. The purpose is not so much to offer a final explanation as to make the most pertinent data readily available for those who wish to search farther for a causality. I am convinced that, the phenomenon being cultural, the explanation must first of all be made in cultural terms, even if it be essentially only a descriptive interpretation. The underlying psychology may ultimately be discoverable; but that will necessarily be later. I have offered an adumbration of an explanation in terms of cultural patterns. This will perhaps be considered insufficient. It does not wholly satisfy me. While we know a good deal in detail about some specific culture patterns, we are only in

* ORIGINALLY PUBLISHED by the University of California Press, reprinted by permission of The Regents of the University of California.

the beginning of understanding of the nature of such patterns; even their theoretical recognition is recent. How some sharply marked patterns in civilization have actually behaved, historically, seems worth knowing as a first empirical step toward understanding; and my main endeavor has been to present organized materials on this behavior.

That this book dealing with data from history should have been written by an anthropologist will perhaps seem fitting to those interested in the development of the two studies. The aim of the work is obviously more or less sociological. The principal current of anthropology, and its soundest findings until now, I believe to be culture-historical. Nevertheless, if we can also generalize validly, it will be most important.

Problem and Procedure

THE UNDERTAKING

✤ Eduard Meyer, by some considered the greatest historian of our time, assigns to anthropology the task of determining the generic or universal features in human history. He accepts, of course, like all historians, what have been called the principles of the continuity or unity and of the uniqueness of history. That is to say, he holds as primary assumptions that every historical phenomenon has antecedents which in turn have antecedents; that it never originates out of nothing; that every effect also becomes a cause or influence; that exact repetition of phenomena is therefore impossible; in short, that all historic events possess individuality or uniqueness while occurring in an interconnected continuum. Beyond this there seem to lie certain forms of happenings which are more or less recurrent or generic, perhaps necessary and universal. These are no longer the province of the historian as such. Formerly, concern with them was left to what was called the philosophy of history—a field of inquiry on the margin of philosophy proper, somewhat sociological in intent but readier than sociology to deal primarily with historical data as such. The significance of Meyer's allocation of the study of the generic or repetitive forms in history to anthropology rather than to "Geschichtsphilosophie" lies in the fact that anthropology is not a philosophical science,

83

but an empirical one; that it has been rather freely admitted by scientists to fall within the domain of natural science; and that its bent, as compared with that of sociology, has been overwhelmingly investigatory and not practical or ameliorative.

On the other side, anthropologists have prevailingly been inclined to construe their discipline as a historical science; at any rate, since about 1890, the majority have come to avow explicitly that the cultural phenomena with which they deal are properly intelligible only in a historic context.

These remarks are made in justification, if such be needed, of an anthropologist's dealing with wholly historical data. The two approaches are closely related. However, they are also indubitably distinct; and the differentiation is of moment—precisely because it is historically founded.

The immediately available data of history normally are records of events, acts performed by persons. From these, plus surviving monuments, works of literature, and the like, the "institutions and manners" or cultures of the past are inferred and reconstructed; and these reconstructions are again used in helping to explain why particular events happened. The historian may make pauses in which he depicts the culture of an area in a period. On the whole, however, these static sections tend to be incidents or interludes. Ordinarily the business of history is the narration of a sequential series of events in their connections or coherences, with culture as a context.

The anthropologist's situation is essentially the reverse: he deals with culture as such, in a context of history. Concerned, not in principle but usually *de facto*, with recordless peoples, the "primitives," he can learn relatively little of particular events among them, and concentrates on the facts and forms of their culture. Are the Dayaks archers, headhunters, weavers, matrilineal, totemic; were the Magdalenians archers, potters, weavers, fishermen? These are the kinds of data which he has developed methods for collecting more or less competently. In what spot or year, and by what individual, pots were first made among a certain tribe, is usually beyond his power of ascertaining; or even the name of the chief who led in a victory over a neighboring tribe, or the date of the fight, unless it occurred within the memory of the living.

True, these differences intergrade. Even the avowedly biographic historian brings in much culture by implication; and an anthropologist who disregarded such historical events as he might learn of would be considered a deficient workman. There is archaeology, of Egypt for instance, from which history with names, acts, dates, and places is reconstructed. There are historians who debate each other's "interpretations" or reconstructions of the socioeconomic pattern of the typical early mediaeval town very much as anthropologists debate whether pyramids and kingship and calendar were or were not imported from Asia into Central America, or whether matrilineal or patrilineal institutions, or totems or moieties, were the earlier in Australia. Nevertheless, using culture as an instrument to infer or understand the sequence of events, or using events to understand culture, are diverse processes of intelligence. Events are specific facts; culture by comparison is a generalized abstraction. History is therefore particular, and scarcely ever has detached itself wholly from individual persons. Anthropology often becomes technically detailed, but it can operate successfully without any knowledge of particular persons. The cultures which it depicts or analyzes are summaries or averages of a large number of individual acts.

It will accordingly be clear why Meyer leaves to anthropology the task of investigating the general or universal forms of human history: such forms are cultural.

The problem I have set myself in this book is an investigation of one of the forms which culture takes. This form is the frequent habit of societies to develop their cultures to their highest levels spasmodically: especially in their intellectual and aesthetic aspects, but also in more material and practical respects. The cultures grow, prosper, and decline, in the opinion of the world. How far they tend to be successful in their several activities simultaneously, or close together, or far apart in time, and how much variation in this regard is of record, is part of the problem. The type of phenomenon has been frequently noted, or has been widely taken for granted; it has not been systematically investigated, so far as I know, by a comparison of all available facts; that is to say, investigated empirically instead of intuitively or *a priori*.

The first question is whether such clusterings or spurts of higher cultural productivity are real or are perhaps only illusions of our minds. Then arises a series of more specific questions. Is there a tendency toward a norm of duration for such successful growths, or anything to show of what the duration is a function? Must the florescence extend over the whole of the culture, or may it be partial? Is there an order, or tendency toward order, for the several activities to come successively to their zeniths? Can a culture pass through a cycle to full decline and then enjoy another cycle of prosperity, or are we in that case dealing with two cultures? Can the cycles or bursts be induced from without, or must they develop from within? Do the peaks tend to come early within growths, toward the end, or is the growth curve most often symmetrical? We have here a whole set of problems, or possible problems, on which there exist abundant data, but of which there has been little systematic comparative research.

It is also evident that this set of problems is only one of a number that confront us in regard to the nature of culture. It confines itself to those cultural productions which seem qualitatively successful to other times and places—which have impressed and commanded a certain respect for their values from other cultures. Besides dealing with cultural quality, the problem deals with its distributions in chronological time and geographical space. But I have deliberately refrained, except incidentally or when necessary, from examining the content of the cultural growth. I have not tried to write a summary or comparative history of philosophy or science or painting with reference to what each civilization achieved in these activities. I have tried to see how far the several civilizations have behaved alike or unlike in the course of producing their highest manifestations in these activities. Nor again, except so far as it seemed necessary, have I dwelt on the sources of the culture material worked into florescences, nor on the influences and stimuli which disparate civilizations received from one another. In short, the characteristic content and specific quality of high cultural developments have been disregarded here, and with them their possible "causes," in favor of their growth configurations—configurations in time, in space, and in degree of achievement. Such a limitation has the merit of focusing attention on certain aspects of the phenomena, and of dealing with comparables, or near-comparables, instead of with everything at once. Obviously, an examination thus limited will not reveal causes. But I cheerfully renounce present search for these, because a clearer and surer understanding of how cultures behave historically seems antecedent to why they behave as they do. The treatment, in short, is behavioristically factual rather than explanatory.

CONCLUSIONS

For convenience, the principal conclusions arrived at in the foregoing pages are summarized.

It is clear that aesthetic and intellectual endeavors resulting in higher values preponderantly realize themselves in temporary bursts, or growths, in all the higher civilizations examined. The same sort of bursts or growths tend to characterize nationalistic development, as expressed in successful political organization and expansion. Whether the phenomenon holds also for wealth and population, is a separate question, which I have not gone into because the data are of a different order and seem much more difficult to acquire over continuous long ranges of history. It seems possible that the behavior of wealth and population may prove different, because these phenomena are naturally expressible quantitatively, whereas the index for those considered is essentially qualitative through the medium of genius. At any rate, genius is one way in which the degree of aesthetic and intellectual achievement can be expressed. The world has, however, never been ready to admit any strong correlation between genius and wealth accumulation; and the peculiarly quantitative consideration of population size is obviously also a distinct matter.

It is entirely conceivable that there may be a connection between growth of population and wealth and the achievement growths which have been analyzed. It would certainly be somewhat difficult to imagine highly cultural achievements reaching their culmination among a population whose size and wealth were consistently declining. No serious long-range and comparative studies appear, however, to have been undertaken on this problem, and it seems wise to defer opinion until they shall have been made.

The tracing of the degree or quality of value growths has been made on the assumption that genius is a fair representative of cultural value. It is the clustering of recognized genius in time and space and common speech which is the basis of the value-growth appraisals which have been outlined in this book.

This implies a definition of genius supplementary to the customary or popular one that a genius is an individual who is eminently superior in his mental endowment. A social definition of genius may also be offered. Geniuses are the indicators of the realization of coherent pattern growths of cultural value.

A corollary is that most of the potential geniuses born are never realized, so far as history or human values are concerned. The supply of genius, physiologically or psychologically speaking, ought to remain essentially constant in any one race within any period which is not unduly long. However, inasmuch as even the peoples possessing higher civilization have produced cultural products of value only intermittently, during relatively small fractions of their time span, it follows that more individuals born with the endowment of genius have been inhibited by the cultural situations into which they were born than have been developed by other cultural situations.

The reason for the transience of high-value patterns is not altogether clear. It is evident that such patterns must be selective and somehow differentiated or specialized. This in turn necessitates that any such pattern fairly early takes a particular direction. The pattern is then gradually pushed to its limits in that direction. These limits may be the limitations of the physical world. But they need not be such. The very selection which at the outset is necessary if a distinctive pattern is to be produced, is almost certain later on to become a limitation. It is then often or normally too late to go back and widen the scope of the pattern without undoing the entire growth which it has achieved. It seems to be historically almost as difficult to reconstitute a pattern fundamentally, or to widen greatly the scope of a growth, as at an earlier stage it is difficult to get a distinctive pattern growth or pattern value started. Not infrequently, when a pattern has attained realization or reached saturation, its limitations appear to be felt and efforts are made to alter or enlarge it. If these efforts take the form of a pause in activity, there may be a reconstitution of energy and direction, with the result that, after a lull, growth is resumed along somewhat new and broader lines. The early eighteenth-century pause in the growth of European science is an illustration of this type of phenomenon.

More often, perhaps, there is no such abatement or recession once a peak of pattern realization has been attained. Endeavors become evident toward strain and rupture of the pattern. The impulses toward change and growth persist, but take the form of extravagance, flamboyance, or alteration for the sake of novelty. At other times these endeavors are repressed, with the result that, change, or at any rate important change, being no longer tolerated, there is no recourse for activity other than in essential repetition, which necessarily brings with it deterioration of quality. This is the condition familiar as Byzantinism. Such Byzantinism need not be permanent, nor need it involve the whole of a civilization. If it remains sufficiently brief, it may behave somewhat like one of the temporary lulls and be followed by a period of renewed activities with more or less reconstituted patterns. If the interval is not too long, and the reconstituted growth reaches higher values than the original one, the type is that of a lull followed by the second phase of a greater growth. If, on the other hand, the interval is longer, and especially if the second-growth pulse fails to reach as high an achievement as the first, the later effort is of the type of an attenuated renaissance episode in a Byzantine decline.

Particular attention has been paid to these lulls and to the pulses or phrases which they separate. Latin literature, with its three or four pulses separated by definite time intervals, is a case in point. So is Egyptian art in a very much longer time span.

In well-unified and well-defined civilizations the configuration of growth and decline may be clean-cut even though marked by several crests. In a multinational civilization like that of Europe, each nation shows its own crests, and at the same time the several culminations replace each other, like instruments in an orchestra, so that there is a larger polyphonic configuration for the supernational civilization as a whole.

There are a number of configurations with several crests, of which the middle one is clearly the highest. In them, the first and last growth pulses partake of the nature of prologue and epilogue; or, pro-dromal and aftermath efforts may be better designations. The total culture history of Spain, and again that of ancient Greece, seem to fall into this form.

The growth curves are sometimes symmetrical like a normal varia-bility curve; sometimes skew, the crest appearing either before or after the middle of the duration. Skew curves are, if anything, more frequent for single activities. The curves for total cultures show some-what more of a tendency toward symmetry, presumably because they are a composite of curves for several activities. There is enough varia-bility to make it uncertain whether growth is typically expressible by a symmetrical normal curve.

The duration is also extremely variable, ranging from as little as thirty or forty years to as much as five hundred or a thousand. On the whole, it can be said that growths tend to be longer in proportion as they produce what posterity has recognized as great values. There are, however, large differences in duration, apart from this consideration. Thus the Sanskrit drama took several times as long to develop and decline as the Elizabethan, even with the Restoration drama counted in as part of the latter. There do seem to be significant national differences. Irrespective of kind of activity, all datable growths in India are slow.

There is no clear evidence of a tendency toward acceleration of growth as we pass from ancient to modern times. Of course, in this connection, comparison would be illegitimate between a culture like that of France, which is only one strand of the larger European culture, and, say, that of India or China, which, culturally speaking, are continental rather than national. Occidental culture as a whole has already developed about as long as ancient and Asiatic ones.

I do not set a norm of duration for the growths of larger civiliza-tions, though the usual estimates of a thousand to fifteen hundred years are probably approximately right as an average. It seems doubt-ful whether any absolute figure can have much meaning: it would be only the doubtfully significant statistical average of a small number of instances. That is, it is uncertain whether duration values *per se* are significant of anything inherent. It seems reasonable that conditions of area, population, and kind of culture developed, which are almost necessarily variable, would be of sufficient influence to prevent any standard duration. The similarity between instances is probably less in tempo than in configuration; and this suggests that the real constants lie in the growth processes involved.

There is an evident tendency for growths in distinct activities to be associated in time, but no clear indication that a successful growth in one activity must be accompanied by growths in other activities. In other words, successful activity growths in one culture may be few or solitary; and many civilizations have failed to attain high achievement in one or another activity. That, on the contrary, growths tend to occur associated may be attributed to the fact that distinctive success in one activity presupposes a high degree of cultural energy, and once this is aroused it is unlikely to remain restricted to a single activity. But again, there is no reason to believe that once such cultural energy is aroused it must necessarily spread to all possible fields of cultural activity, since it is notorious that civilizations differ in their interests and emphases. The most marked example toward close clustering in time of the culminations in diverse activities is furnished by Greek civilization. Here the unusually small population involved may have been the cause; not only the number in any one city-state, but the total number of Greeks, was small. Our familiarity with Greek history has, then, served to set up this case as a type. Actually, it is almost unique in its degree of simultaneity of activity developments.

There is no marked evidence of an inherent order of succession in which the several cultural activities develop. So far as there is a tendency for sculpture to precede painting, the cause lies not in anything cultural, but in the fact that sculpture is the physically simpler art. The tendency toward sequence, if there is one, lies in the laws of nature rather than in some law of culture. Science possesses certain inherent relations with philosophy, and philosophy again with religion, and religion again with art. But these relations have been worked out quite diversely in their cultural manifestations. Science,

91

philosophy, and religion impinge on one another psychologically, but their expressions in cultural growth do have manifold, and may have minimal, relations.

Religion, however, in general precedes aesthetic and intellectual developments of note, and a history of the arts is frequently one of gradual emancipation from religion as they attain their culminations. This relation appears to inhere in the definition of the concepts. We hardly recognize philosophy and science as such until they have reached a certain level of development and organization. Below this threshold, which we do not avow but nevertheless recognize, we tend to treat these activities as nonexistent. Somewhat similarly for the arts, though there the threshold is a certain degree of quality attainment. Religion, on the other hand, is more or less omnipresent. At any rate, we tend to deal with it as if there were no corresponding threshold. The result is that when we begin our consideration of florescences in art, science, or philosophy, it is against a background of preëxisting religion, which has inevitably had relation with the formative or prethreshold stages of the other activities. Nevertheless, the criterion of emancipation of these activities from religious influence has a certain empirical value of defining their degree of development.

To the question whether there may be national florescences without accompanying cultural ones, or vice versa, the answer must be yes, although such happenings are rare in history. It is evident that ethnic or national energy and cultural energy are related but are not the same thing. Ethnic energy may be conceived of as potential cultural energy, or as cultural energy expressed in simple and immediate forms, with more emphasis on specifically social than on specifically cultural ends.

Of some importance is the relation of cultural content, which is fairly readily expressible quantitatively through descriptive enumeration, and cultural forms or patterns, which we apperceive qualitatively and which seem quantitatively expressible only by the indirect method of estimating the rating of genius. The difficulty of dealing with the relation lies in the fact that culture content and culture form occur only in association with each other, and are therefore imperfectly distinguishable. Here is a fundamental problem of anthropology which still awaits most of its solution. It will probably be conceded that more growth of value can be attained on a larger body of content or material. Content tends to grow cumulatively, whereas forms are more or less predetermined by their origins. The result is that a certain set of forms may be realized or fulfilled while the content of the culture is still growing. In that event, the consequence is a partial dissolution with reconstitution on an ampler scale; after which the patterns may proceed in a new growth or pulse. Fourteenth- and fifteenth-century transalpine Europe is an example of such an interval between pattern growths, while culture content was rapidly expanding.

The more insular cultures, like those of Japan and England, seem to possess a somewhat retarded growth, which, however, is steadier and less intermittent than that of corresponding mainland cultures exposed to more numerous and sharper competitive contacts.

Geographically, a radiating spread of culture growth can usually be traced from a first hearth or focus over the larger area finally occupied. This is in accord with what anthropologists have again and again noted in regard to specific diffusions. They have, it is true, mostly dealt with items of culture content; but the same process of spread seems to apply more or less to culture patterns and values. The spread is perhaps most often from the center outward; but the original focus may be situated on a geographical margin and the spread therefore be fanwise rather than radiating. If so, the focus is likely to lie on a frontier exposed to foreign stimulation. It is also possible for much of the periphery to develop first, and the remaining spread then to be centripetal.

Another type of centripetal change sometimes occurs during the decline of a large cviilization: it then shrinks upon itself; as Mediterranean or Classic civilization, after having spread from the Hellenic area to include the Roman West, retracted later within its original Greek limits, the West relapsing into barbarism.

Cultural death has here been construed only as the death of particular cultures or forms of culture; that is, as the replacement of particular patterns, which may be of higher value, by other patterns.

The question whether a whole culture can die of itself through internal causes or inherent aging is not answered.

A final review listing of such genius as has occurred in isolation shows such occurrence to be definitely rare, and justly to be designated as exceptional. The methodological assumption on which this volume rests seems therewith to be vindicated, at any rate approximately. A derivative corollary is that we human beings are, at least so far as our accomplishments go, the products of our cultures much more than we ordinarily recognize.

As for findings that are universal, or such as might express a general sociology of human history, this investigation has attained only to approximations, though some of these may stimulate further inquiry. My own feeling is that the growth-configuration approach results rather in a multiplicity of specific historic findings. These are occasionally new, more frequently a shifted emphasis or realigned interpretation. And the endless events of history are lifted out of their level of near-uniformity into organized relief, by an attitude which consciously recognizes pattern-growth configurations in their space-time relations as well as in their value relations.

An Anthropologist Looks at History is a posthumously published collection of essays, one of which provided the title for the book. Four are presented here because they deal with historical changes including the more recent periods. They are: "An Anthropologist Looks at History," "History and Anthropology in the Study of Civilizations," "The Personality of Anthropology," "On Human Nature."

An Anthropologist Looks at History *

✠ The writing of history is perhaps the oldest of scholarly pursuits. Moreover, it has persisted with minimal alteration for more than

* Reprinted by permission from *Pacific Historical Review*, Vol. XXVI, No. 3, pp. 281–87.

two thousand years, and across change of language, ever since Herodotus and Thucydides and the even earlier days of the Chinese. History therefore contains much that is art: the narration of significant events in literary prose. This is evident further in the fact that the great historians are also, in the main, great writers. They write the language of total and dignified communication of their day, without technical terms or jargon, less even than philosophers employ. And they operate with a nontechnical psychology, a psychology of generic experience and common understanding. And similarly they operate with an untechnical common man's causality, intelligible on its face; and a similar common morality. Basically, this still holds true as it did two or more millennia ago.

Anthropology is not wholly a historical science, but large areas of it are historical in interest and intent. Prehistory is an allied pursuit of knowledge in the classification of disciplines customary in Europe and an outright part of anthropology in American usage. And prehistoric archaeology is of course, in its aim at least, merely history pushed back of writing and documents, whether in Sumeria, Japan, Morocco, South Africa, the Pueblo Indian Southwest, or Peru. Names and identifiable individuals are of necessity missing when the record is of preliterate times; specific events are determinable only now and then; but the residue of possible findings is a sort of condensed social history. We learn of buildings, artifacts, arts, about bones of animals hunted for daily living and of animals reared domesticated. Human bones give us not only some glimpses of the prevalent physique, but methods of burial, and sometimes clear indications of classes and economic differences. If carvings are cultish, they allow of inferences as to religious beliefs and practices; so do temples, shrines, preserved offerings. Excavations and records, made and kept intensively enough, lead to conclusions as to size of community, number of communities in a period, and other demographic information on populations whose ethnic name may be wholly unknown, and whom the prehistorian may have to christen. We know in some cases the approximate proportion of males and females, of aged and adults and children in a population, and we may be able to speculate with some show of evidence how far its particular distribution of age and sex was due to disease, war, malnutrition, or human sacrifice. All this is most eminently social or cultural history, even though of nameless peoples. In fact, if his luck with the spade is good, the archaeologist may come to control fuller data on daily life and custom than annalists conscious chiefly of kings' glories and battles have left to the historiographer as data for some nominally literate period or country.

Archaeological data resolve naturally into narrative. The very first discoveries in an area may be felt merely as new, different, surprising, or otherwise emotionally toned. But as soon as the remains of the past vary within an area, it is evidently probable that they come from different periods, and intellectual curiosity will try to arrange them in their order of age. Stylistic comparisons, or sometimes typological, sooner or later give clues or indications as to sequences. If ornamented pottery was produced, the task is usually made much easier. Clay is a virtually imperishable material, it is likely to be fairly abundant, it is unusually plastic in its manufacture, and thus if it is decorated its style almost never stands still very long. Many a sequence of pottery styles have been worked out with a fair probability of historic authenticity for societies whose absolute dates we know as little as their names or origins.

The final validation of the archaeologist's reconstructions of the past is by the minutely careful excavation of stratified sites—levels of objects of different style superposed in the sequence of time as they were laid down; like the successive cities of Troy, or the levels of Cnossos. This is the clinching proof. There is an element of luck in the finding of such sites. Peoples of later periods often started to build and live and leave refuse at new sites rather than settle where their predecessors had operated; but not always so; and while discovery of the strategic key site may not be immediate, it is usually located within a generation or two of problem-conscious exploration.

Ways have lately been devised of attaching approximate absolute dates to events and periods established by prehistorians as having occurred in a given relative sequence. Thereby such findings are brought strictly into the compass of history. Dendrochronology or tree-ring dating was the first of these technical methods; it is fully successful, so far, only in certain areas of subnormal rainfall and for certain species of trees. It has carried us back, in our Pueblo-Anasazi Southwest, nearly two thousand years. Carbon-14 determinations reach back from ten to perhaps twenty times as far as dendrochronology. They have solved some chronological problems, have complicated others. They have perhaps helped most in the precopper range of time, and in North America they seem to have halved the estimated time elapsed since the end of the last glaciation, thus yielding a closer tie-up of geology with human prehistory.

Original ethnographic inquiries made by the field anthropologist among surviving native peoples are less patently historical in their immediate results, because of the surprisingly brief historic memories of most nonliterate populations. But here, too, systematic comparison sooner or later leads to perspectives of time depth for institutions, arts, rituals, as for ethnic groups themselves. The ethnographic approach is definitely slower than prehistoric excavation in converting its result into chronologically firm culture history; but it gives a fuller and more living picture because less has been lost by the decays of time.

I think that most anthropologists would look on history as being a realm adjoining their own country, speaking a somewhat different dialect, governed by laws similar in intent though often variant in detail, and connected by innumerable ties of activity across their joint frontier.

I see human history or historiography as a specialization within a much broader and more general intellectual activity: namely, that of viewing any and all phenomena in the universe "historically"—in their flow through time. Just as there legitimately exists "social" and "intellectual" and "economic" history alongside "political" history of the peoples who have left us written documents, so there exists a potential history—in fact an existent and progressive history—of the nonliterate human populations whom we know through their settlements, burials, artifacts, and refuse. There is, further, a history of life. This is the story of biological evolution, as it is now known, both in general outline and—in spots, in considerable detail—from the records of fossils, supplemented by comparisons with the array of living forms of animals and plants. The internal structure and physiology of these living forms being known or ascertainable, they help to illuminate dark areas in the inferences from the fossils. Beyond that there is obviously also a history of our planet as a body; a history of the solar system; and a possible history of galaxies and the universe. These remoter histories may be more largely potentially inferable than already ascertained; but we are here considering what can be done rather than what has been done. And at that, the achieved is considerable—enough to show that we are already far beyond mere vague hopes and dreams.

In short, every part and aspect of our universe has a history which is gradually recoverable. Or let us call it "a historical approach" to the phenomena of primitive man, of life, of the earth, of our solar system. The substitute phrase is suggested to guard against anyone's being worried at stretching the term *history* to a meaning beyond that of the conventional historiography of the written-record-leaving portion of humanity.

My point is that all these interests and inquiries, so far as they aim at narratively understanding a class of phenomena in their flow through time, are of one general kind, of which documented historiography is one particular example, though by far the oldest established example. Why historiography originated two millennia or more earlier than a historical approach in other fields of intellectual inquiry seems to be not at all an insoluble problem, but it is definitely more than can be answered here today. Yet that it originated earlier is an unquestionable fact; and the time available to me may suffice to show, not why human historiography was early, but that the development of the historical approach in other fields of knowledge was on the whole surprisingly late; and perhaps why it was so.

A science like astronomy today has a double aspect. It studies with accuracy and precision the processes that are going on in the universe of the heavens; and it reconstructs the events that have happened in the development of the stars. The Babylonians already, and the Greeks not long after, knew the motions of the planets, the recurring motions and aberrations of the moon, the latitudes and approximate size of the earth. The revolutions of the heavenly bodies were recurrent; they were repeated over and over, identically and endlessly; except for this internal motion, the universe seemed static. It did not appear to have had a history. It seems not even to have occurred to the Greeks that the universe might have had a development. Such motions as they determined and measured, in the great machine of the planetary system, impressed them by their regularity: they were fixed notions: they showed how immutable the machine was; and what is immutable has no history.

Such was still the assumption of Copernicus, two thousand years later. It was not till the eighteenth century that La Place—and the philosopher Kant—originated nebular hypotheses as conjectural histories of how our and other solar systems developed. It took a century and a half of improvement of telescopes and chronometers before enough data had been accumulated on the distances and motions of fixed stars for such hypothetical reconstructions of the history of our universe to be felt as needed and to be devised. In the nineteenth century the spectroscope, photography, and astrophysics have piled up further knowledge, and the histories have been remodeled accordingly.

In other words, here is a precision science, astronomy, quantitative from the first, and cumulatively gaining range and accuracy, which began to see sequential and developmental problems in its material and to find historical answers to them only after more than two millennia of activity.

It was as late as the eighteenth century also that the essentially historical science of geology began dimly to glimpse some ends and tatters of events of our planet's history, in the vulcanist versus neptunist controversy. It was only in the nineteenth century that a reasonably complete sequential series of geologic periods could be laid down.

Biology remained in its totality an ahistorical science until 1859. The efforts of Erasmus, Darwin, Lamarck, and other scattered heretics failed to swerve either botany or zoölogy from regarding their phenomena as essentially fixed and changeless—barring the accidents of occasional catastrophic blottings-out. The entire ramified history of life on earth, as it is accepted by biological consensus today, has been less than a century in its working out. Being worked out as a *story*, that is; for the systematic *classification* of life forms that had been made by and since Linnaeus, supplemented by the discoveries of a hitherto dateless palaeontology, proved to be immediately convertible into a history of life on earth as soon as biologists were ready to think in terms of sequences of events as well as relationship of forms.

It appears from these examples that historiography—the telling of human recorded history—is the only history which is genuinely old as an accepted pursuit; and that the historical sciences are definitely newcomers, both as compared with historiography on the one hand and with mathematics, physics, and astronomy on the other.

Historiography has so consistently been nontheoretical, unwilling or unable to abstract process from out of its phenomena on any notable scale, as to cause the widely prevalent view that history as an endeavor and pursuit *must* be something fundamentally distinct from natural science; or that, if in some measure a science, it was a science of an older and simpler order, forever attached to its phenomena instead of advancing from them to systematic generalization, abstraction, and theory.

Such a view receives surface support from the fact that, as regards both methods and devices used and concepts attained, historiography has essentially stood still while mathematics, astronomy, and physics have cumulatively progressed.

However, if the historical approach were in itself of a simpler order or lower potential than that of systematically conceptual science, we should hardly have historical astronomy, historical geology, and historical biology developing only within the last two centuries.

Accordingly, our problem must evidently be approached in some other way.

I would suggest that in subhuman fields of nature it is naturally easy to recognize repetitive regularities; such as the seasons and the heavenly bodies; the exemplars of a species; such as, also, falling bodies, the action of levers which we daily handle, in fact possess in our limbs; or liquids finding their level. These recurrent regularities in themselves point to law; and the sciences first emanating from them are nomothetic. Natural science thus tends to begin with the static or with motion within a static frame. The longer range macrodynamisms that transform a gaseous nebula into stars and planets, that gradually transmute one kind or order of living things into another, do not obtrude in everyday observation. In fact, they cannot be dealt with, other than by mere speculation, until large masses of observations have been accumulated or wholly new methods of observation have been devised. Hence in the natural sciences of subhuman phenomena the historical approach comes late; it is possible only after much development.

But in men's observations of one another, there is little to lead them to concentrate on recurring regularity or to induce notions of fixity or law. Everyone develops, with the very experience of living, his own practical skills of interpreting and dealing with other human beings, as a practical necessity; but if in spite of this psychology remains the least organized and theoretically least productive of the major sciences, this fact suggests strongly that its material is scientifically the most difficult and recalcitrant. Historiography, however, while it constantly employs, unorganized, experientially derived psychological judgments—practical judgments—does not really deal directly with "psyches," as psychology does, but with the multiform actions or events due to these psyches or persons. And in concerning itself with them, it tends to avoid the regular and the expectable, or tacitly takes them for granted, and concentrates on the singular and the unusual, on the stirring and dramatic; and, as it attains to more sophistication, on the significant and effective.

Perhaps if we had a theoretical science of psychology as organized, efficient, and productive on its own level, as are physics, chemistry, and biochemistry, it would be followed before long by a historical psychology corresponding to historical astronomy, geology, and biology. What form such a historical psychology would take, I do not pretend to picture. But it would be interesting to know how far such a scientifically historical psychology would turn out to resemble the history of historians or how far it might transcend it as something radically different in attack, manner, and product.

Alfred Kroeber

History and Anthropology in the Study of Civilizations*

SOME GENERAL DIFFERENCES OF HISTORY AND ANTHROPOLOGY

✤ Differences in subject.—History deals with events, with emphasis on uniqueness and on change. Events are the actions of human beings, individually, in groups, or in masses. Anthropology deals primarily with culture, with emphasis on the expectable, on its relatively permanent forms. These are two separate, selective focuses, though many data may be shared.

Differences in method.—History is narrative primarily, with optional halts for "topical" description. This is true by common consent definition. Anthropology is perhaps primarily descriptive (ethnology, ethnography) but also narrative if the data allow—often in most prehistory and archaeology.

Differences in sources.—History relies on written documents, ultimately. Anthropology characteristically "makes" its documents, elicits them in face-to-face situations of oral communication with informants; plus of course observation. In archaeology, physical anthropology, observation is primary.

The face-to-face contacts are almost enforced with primitive cultures, and many have contributed to the further preoccupation of ethnology with the primitive. At any rate, anthropologists are often considered romantics among men of science.

Note:—Here, and in what follows, the word "Anthropology" is used in its older and original sense of a widely inclusive science, attempting to understand and interrelate all principal aspects of mankind, with central emphasis on man's most distinctive product, culture. The other social sciences are concerned with particular aspects of human culture: social, economic, political, personal. Anthropology alone tries to deal with culture as such, both through

* READ BEFORE the Comparative Civilizations Symposium at the Center for Advanced Study in the Behavioral Sciences, Stanford, California, spring, 1958, reprinted with the approval of Mrs. Theodora Kroeber Quinn.

total descriptions and through conceptualization, "theoretically." Associated with understanding of culture are knowledge of its past (prehistory); of the most autonomous special sector of culture, namely language; and even of the racial physiques and bodies of men that have produced culture (physical anthropology). The two first of these associated studies—archaeology and linguistics—are usually considered humanities, when pursued in isolation; analogously, racial anthropology is obviously also part of biology. No other social science allows its operations to extend so far into frankly humanistic or natural science. This anomaly of anthropology is undoubtedly connected with its other anomalous feature in the social sciences, its holistic instead of segmental interest in culture. Its holism is almost certainly what for several generations kept anthropology from attempting practical applications.

This is the older and most characteristic form of anthropology, which I am comparing with history.

A more special development began as "functionalism" in England about forty years ago and has gradually assumed the name "Social Anthropology." This sometimes shifts the focus from holistic culture to its societal segment (Radcliffe-Brown) or sometimes uses culture as a base or background against which societal structure and dynamics, interpersonal interactions, and modifications of culture resulting from societal and personal situations, are examined (Firth and others). It is evident that social anthropology is much less anomalous as a social science than was the older anthropology; it is no longer culture-centered and it is no longer actively holistic. In fact, in England, social anthropology, prehistory, and physical anthropology are increasingly prosecuted as separate disciplines, as compared with Tylor's days or even Marett's; and linguistics is not pursued at all, except as a tool, or as a wholly independent study. In the United States, there is little tendency toward separatism, and cultural ("ethnological") and social anthropology are practiced side by side, sometimes even without much awareness of difference.

It is clear that the close-range focus of social anthropology does not encompass large changes and that so far as the results are historical they are characteristically short-term. A comparison with historiography would therefore be limited essentially to "contemporary history."

For this reason the comparisons here made with history are of the culture-centered, holistic, and long-range anthropology which first crystallized out as a discipline and has determined its characteristic trend.

SOME GENERIC SIMILARITIES OF HISTORY AND ANTHROPOLOGY

1. Histories generally began on a national, perhaps provincial, basis, but early showed some leanings to being international within a period (Polybius) or civilization, or even to covering all known time and area ("world history"). Anthropological inquiry also varies in range from intensive tribal studies to synthetic ethnographies of the world, and to disquisitions on the nature and properties of culture in general. Both disciplines can take on the long-range and wide view, or the close-up and detailed; both may be holistic but are not necessarily so.

There is one area in which they meet: that of comparative culture history. This involves the comparative running down, across nations and civilizations, of some segment of human activity—a religious form, a mechanical invention, a technological art, a game or an etiquette, an iconography, a philosophical idea, or a symbol. These may be shared by great civilizations with lowly tribal cultures; and the historian of science or art, the Sinologist, classicist, or mediaevalist, share in the search with ethnologist and archaeologist.

2. Unique formulations predominate in history as in anthropology. Generalizations are fluid, not strict laws; results stress significances rather than strict casual determinations.

The following may seem to contradict what has just been said above about holistic tendencies. Anthropologists' descriptions of particular cultures emphasize their distinctness from others, their peculiarities. What cultures share with one another tends to be dealt with more succinctly.

Most anthropologists are skeptical about "laws." Boas' early hopes of finding them were later given up, and the possibility denied. Historians and anthropologists are almost unanimous on this point.

3. Contextual coherence is a sign of good historiography, of good ethnology, and most markedly of good linguistic description, language being perhaps the most autonomous part of culture. "Coherence" is in terms of the whole and of the parts.

4. There exists a great world-wide web of permanent inventions, contacts, and spreads of culture components. The content of all civilizations and cultures is mostly of extraneous origin. More has seeped in from abroad than was devised at home. The alphabet, money, chess and cards, paper and printing are examples.

For many world-wide items of civilization we can now prove a single origin and spread. Some years ago Kroeber used the Greek word *Oikumenê*—the part of the inhabited world in which civilization existed—to denote the area of greatest concentration of this shared content of culture in Europe, Asia, and North Africa; exchange has gone on for thousands of years. Native Australia and America participated less. Even in the Old Stone Age long-range diffusions are evident.

5. These commonalties are not psychologically derivable (from "human nature," as used to be thought) but are products of historical events.

The time, place, and circumstances of the origin and further development of any institution, invention, or cultural form must be considered a legitimate and potentially soluble problem of inquiry through analytic comparison.

6. Civilizations are construable as precipitates of the events of history.

Inventions, customs, codes and values of civilization in an area are the residues of historic (and subliminally historic) events as these accumulate.

7. Culture is the common frontier of anthropology with historiography and its branches such as Sinology, Egyptology, etc. This holds especially for remote and ancient civilizations.

8. Anthropology is ready to help interweave all data on culture into a history of human culture; but it cannot adequately do so alone.

There is a vital need for professionally equipped experts in the various fields. China, the Islamic world, ancient Egypt, etc. have such experts. And as the desire to achieve the larger goal becomes widespread, the contacts of anthropology with these segments of scholarship will increase.

9. To achieve the larger goal is not an impossible task—biology serves as an encouraging example.

In two centuries biologists have worked out a coherent, reasonably reliable, and still growing history of life on earth ("evolution"). They have done this largely by trusting each other—by having common methods, a common front of attack though on many sectors. They have woven a million different species—each a biological "invention" —into a meaningful scheme and history.

True, the task is simpler for biologists, because biological evolution is irreversible: a branching tree, with all flow one way. In human culture innovations are intricately recombined. Similarity may be due to common origin or to secondary interinfluences often difficult to separate. On the other hand, historians of culture have the advantages of vast bodies of direct documentation such as biologists lack.

10. Essentially, the comparative study of civilization is the history of all human cultures in their interrelations.

To many of us it seems desirable to have an over-all or macro-view of this totality.

11. The model of such study is not in physics but in historiography and in natural history.

Philosophers have tended to set up mechanistic physics as the model for all science. This is unfortunate and belated. Hugh Miller and Hans Reichenbach both of the University of California, Los Angeles, are honorable exceptions.

12. The finding of pattern relations in context constitutes the essence of the historic approach.

The pattern relationship must be sought primarily in *natural* context, not in the artificial, isolated ("controlled") environment of experiment.

In fact, experiment is of course in the nature of things ordinarily impossible as regards the past, alike in the history of men, of civilizations, and of animal and plant development. This does not denigrate inquiry into these fields; it merely means that inquiry must be pursued by methods different from those of the laboratory.

THE HISTORY OF CIVILIZATION

There appear to be several ways of perceiving and presenting the history of civilization.

(a) One way selects and connects the culminating points of successive civilizations, on the basis of the influence they have had on later civilizations and ultimately on our own of here and now. Contributions of the past which are not actively effective today are very lightly sketched in or are wholly omitted. The story begins with the Stone Ages, goes on to the emergence of metals, cities, and writing in the Ancient Near East, then via Hebrews and Mycenaeans to Greeks, next of course Rome, then Mediaeval and Modern Europe. China and India hardly contribute to the dominant culture of today. Islam impinged from Mohammed to the Crusades, but since then can be virtually ignored, as can be pre-Mohammedan Arabia. Byzantium long seemed a wholly dead end of only antiquarian interest in the history of civilization; but since Russia has entered the competition for world dominance, Byzantine history reacquires a certain significance as an antecedent of Russia.

It is evident that this is a broadened variation of the "succession of empires" form of general history, which also snaked its way through history and geography by connecting the culminations.

This form of general history also finds a parallel in the popular story of biological evolution, with "ages" of culminating invertebrates, fishes, reptiles, mammals, and man.

(b) Biological evolution as viewed by and for biologists is less selective, and aims to give some account of and place for every novel phylum or originating line of development, irrespective of its dominance or success. Echinoderms and mammals receive treatment proportionate to the array of diversity they have achieved; among the chordates, the primitive or regressive lancelets, tunicates and lampreys get their modest but due place alongside the immensely more successful vertebrates, and mollusks are accorded consideration, instead of losing it, precisely because they embody a highly divergent sideline, though without important successors. The treatment, in fine, is strictly and totally comparative rather than selective.

We have as yet no successful histories of civilization on this plan,

107

which would for instance not merge the account of Tibetan culture in that of India (or of China) but would emphasize also its original and its achieved distinctive features, such as a new form of Buddhism which showed its viability by successful export to Mongolia. Historians have been trained toward selectiveness; anthropologists have not been sufficiently trained in narrative. There have been reasonably systematic world ethnographies for more than a century, since Klemm, Waitz, and Prichard, but they have hardly risen above description.

The balanced comparative total history of human culture remains to be written. There is no reason why it should not be successfully accomplished, through a succession of individual tries, by scholars aware of the pitfalls of ethnocentricity and a too-great selectivity.

(c) A third procedure would be less a "history" than a "comparative anatomy" of recurrent characteristic crises or institutions or style phases viewed cross-culturally: revolutions (Brinton), feudalism (Coulborn), archaism (Flinders Petrie). This method compares "organs" rather than "organisms," aspects of cultures rather than total cultures.

THE HISTORIC APPROACH IN SCIENCE GENERALLY

This section differs from the preceding ones in having no specific reference either to "history" as a specific discipine (historiography) or to anthropology. It discusses "historicity" in the sciences generally: a historic approach, a diachronic aim.

1. Ordinary history in the conventional sense, history of notable human acts or events, narrated in the order in which they occurred, is perhaps the earliest body of organized knowledge. It originated fairly soon after the invention of writing in Mesopotamia, Egypt, and China, was taken over by other peoples as they learned to write, including the Hebrews, who gave it a theocratic instead of dynastic slant, and experienced a culmination in Athens of the fifth century B.C. in the still living histories of Herodotus, Thucydides, and Xenophon. These constitute the earliest corpus of organized human knowledge which remains alive and is still read for its intrinsic interest today.

Its subject matter of course is the doings of men, not the events or order of nature. It would be extreme to say that Greek fifth-century history—or the somewhat later history of Ssu-ma Ch'ien—achieved everything that historians of today accomplish. But it accomplished astonishingly much; and its writers continue to be revered as masters today. These early great historians and their immediate Roman imitators are closer to their modern successors in what they achieved, than are ancient scholars and scientists in any other field of knowledge and scholarship.

2. Other branches of Greek "science," in the widest sense of the word, as for instance Sarton employs it, reached their peak development later than the Greek florescence of history. In the lifetime of Thucydides, Greek mathematics was still more than a century from achieving the completion of even its first stage, namely geometry under Euclid; astronomy and physics required two centuries to reach their apogee under Hipparchus and Archimedes; in other words, historiography, qualitative and diachronic, arrived at fundamental maturity earlier than did quantitative and synchronic natural science. This is a cardinal and really remarkable fact, especially in view of the subsequent career of total science.

It seems fair to construe ancient physics and mathematics as essentially synchronic. While they determined recurrent events, they found these occurring not in sequences but in an order which transcended sequence and therefore was essentially above time. True, it had become possible to predict certain future events; but this was precisely because their cycles of recurrence were by eternal law and therefore changeless and timeless.

3. After this, human *scientia* stood nearly still for almost exactly two thousand years, as regards its essential method. Historiography widened its scope but claimed no basically more advanced procedures. Mathematics, astronomy, and physics shone with Copernicus, Galileo, Descartes, and Newton, but their basic orientation was still toward eternal fixities into which time entered only as a measure of repetitive recurrence.

It was only about two hundred years ago that we find the first beginnings of an interest in long-range temporal and non-repetitive events of nature. It was the same eighteenth-century Laplace that completed the mechanistic understanding of our solar system, who also went beyond this in asking how this so regularly functioning system came about, and propounded an answer as to the origin in one version of the nebular hypothesis: Kant evolved another version; the answers are a classic example of the principle of the simultaneity of discoveries and inventions of fundamentally new ideas. At least, a new type of question was being asked about the solar system, and before long about our galaxy and the universe. The discovery of the enormously long orbits of some comets pushed thinking in the same direction. So did the penetration of more powerful telescopes. We ask today whether the universe is expanding or contracting—in which direction it is changing, instead of trying to delimit its changeless fixity. Astronomy has become recognized as a "historical science."

Other historical sciences of nature have developed without much in the way of ancient antecedents: geology, for instance, whose present foundations began to be laid in the late eighteenth century and took shape in the nineteenth.

Biology goes back in some measure to Aristotle, but as a wholly fixed order of life. The eighteenth century launched a systematic classification of living forms under Linnaeus, and then a beginning of physiology which led on into biochemistry; but both these still dealt with static or recurrent conditions. It was not until Darwin—just about a century ago—that the jam was broken, and life forms were seen to have had flow, origins and development, an evolution, and that biology was recognized as possessing a historical as well as a nomothetic aspect.

Still later, genetic biology began with the discovery of "laws of heredity." Yet less than sixty years have sufficed to reveal the extreme complexity of these laws and to shift prime interest from them to the mutations which alter the laws and bring change into the history of life.

It is plain that natural science has developed more diachronic concern, more of the longer historical approach in its interests and repertory, in the last two centuries than in the two millennia before. Instead of historical orientation being a sign of immaturity of development in science, we might almost affirm that natural sciences require a certain maturity before they *can* develop historical orientation.

4. Why should this be so?

One thinks first of Biblical orthodoxy. But Greek science was just as static as was Christian. And literalistic fundamentalism probably actually grew during the nineteenth century as it felt the tide rising around its Mosaicism, somewhat as the twentieth-century Dayton trials high-lighted its final protest.

More likely, religious dogma merely reinforced a deeper pervasive fear of flux as against fixity, fear of an unstable past and therefore unstable future replacing the comfort of eternal repetitiveness. Even the intellectual problems of a world forever spinning in its ordained place are simpler and easier than those of an embarcation on the boundless unknown. At any rate, the fixities and regularities were the first worked out, they were verifiable, and they came to seem very precious. By contrast, the historical approach in natural science involves fluidity, change, complexity, the continued facing of a penumbra of uncertainty.

5. Also contrastively, the historical approach in science presupposes a vast body of systematized knowledge to operate with. It is doubtful whether even the Greeks would have been interested in such a body of information, or have known how to organize it. The revolutions of the heavenly bodies are after all rather few, quite patent, and relatively simple to determine with surprising accuracy, once observations are patiently accumulated over a few generations, as is shown by Mesopotamian, Egyptian, and Mayan astronomy and calendry. The Greeks had observed fossil seashells on mountainsides, and rivers visibly building up their deltas. But it did not occur to them to attack the problems of mountain formation, of erosion, of tracing sequence by succession of strata, of comparing the strata of different regions. Most of the data resulting from inquiry into such problems would have seemed to them to be lacking in intellectual interest, to be merely informational and anecdotal: they did not integrate either with geometry or with virtue. Such would at any rate have been the attitude of Socrates and Plato. It was only the occasional Greek like Herodotus and Aristotle who was genuinely curious about natural

phenomena in general. The civilization as a whole was incurious: it never developed Aristotle's beginnings either in comparative zoölogy or in comparative politics.

The historical interpretation of nature presupposes two conditions. The first is a willingness to deal with becoming as well as being, with flow as well as fixity. The second is the possession of, or the willingness to assemble, an adequately large and growing body of compared knowledge, of information in its natural context. Such a corpus is indispensable for understanding the history equally of the stellar universe, our earth, life upon it, or its human culture. Without such a series of corpuses, and a willingness to examine and organize each one comparatively, there can be no historic interpretation of nature on any of its levels; there can be only pseudohistoric guesses.

6. As regards civilizations or human culture, we have in hand a fair beginning of such a corpus. More data would help, but the need is primarily for more fruitful and reliable comparison of what is already known. There has really been very little attempt at basic classification of civilizations, either of their diachronic courses or of their synchronic anatomies, functions, and generic properties. There have been some intuitive stabs, exaggerations, identifications by formula. Even these have their value as first endeavors that may have to be largely rejected but which may enable later tries to lay securer foundations; and in that light they will be examined next time. But it is clear that most understanding of these matters is still unachieved. Yet there is no reason to fear that it will remain unachievable. In proportion as we recognize both the merits and the limitations of our predecessors, we are enabled to move beyond them.

The Personality of Anthropology *

❖ To define or characterize the personality or individuality of anthropology, I will start from a paradox.

When we compare anthropology and sociology, it is astonishing how alike they prove to be in their general assumptions and basic

* Reprinted by permission from the Kroeber Anthropological Society *Papers*, No. 19, pp. 1–6.

theory, and how diverse they yet are in most of what *de facto* they do or occupy themselves with.

Sociologists and anthropologists agree in dealing with sociocultural phenomena autonomously. Sociocultural data rest on biotic and individual psychic factors, of course, and are therefore limited by them; but they are not derivable or constructively explicable from them. The analysis and understanding of sociocultural phenomena must be made first of all in terms of sociocultural structure and process: "social facts," Durkheim called them; Spencer, "superorganic" effects; Tylor, "culture." As regards man, his societies always exist in association with a culture; his cultures, with a society. A particular study can abstract from the social aspects of a situation to investigate the cultural aspects; or the reverse; or it can deal with the interaction of the social and cultural aspects. This is common doctrine of the two sciences; and in contrast with what they share, it is really a minor matter that sociologists show a propensity to focus their interest on social data, structure, and process, but anthropologists on cultural.

In fact we can go farther. The basic assumptions and principles shared by sociology and anthropology are virtually the only *general* theory existing in that area which it has become customary to call "social science."

Economics, politics, jurisprudence obviously concern themselves with specific facets of society and culture instead of their totality. Psychology is of course basically oriented toward individuals, or *the* individual, much as is biology; social psychology represents a secondary extension, in the development of which sociology was about as important, at least in our own country, as was psychology itself. The classical economic theory was formulated earlier than sociocultural. This was possible because it applied to only one special part of the sociocultural totality: it was also a well-insulated model, whose effectiveness rested upon the assumption that economic phenomena could profitably be considered in a virtual vacuum; if motivations had now and then to be admitted, common-sense psychology was sufficient.

Not only do sociology and anthropology then essentially share their basic theory, but this theory is the only holistic one yet evolved for the sociocultural realm.

113

In view of this sharing of their basic concepts, it is remarkable how preponderantly sociology and anthropology do *not* share the areas which they work and the methods by which they work them.

Most conspicuous, of course, is the virtually total neglect by sociology of several of the fields which between them constitute probably the majority of the area operated in by anthropology.

These fields are: physical anthropology (a most unfortunate name, but this is not the occasion to try to revise it); archaeology and prehistory; linguistics, general, descriptive, and historical; culture history; primitive ethnology; and the folk ethnography of peasantry in civilized countries as it is pursued in Europe. Sociologists do not hesitate to use results obtained in these subdisciplines; but they rarely make intrinsic contributions to them, as all anthropologists do in one or more fields.

Now it is notable that with one exception—that of primitive ethnography—all these fields are, however, shared by anthropologists with non-anthropologists. Physical anthropology of course is only a fragment of biology, and whether a worker is physical anthropologist, anatomist, or human geneticist is largely a matter of what he calls himself or of job classification. Archaeology inevitably runs into art and classics—there even are notable departments named "Art and Archaeology," and our Archaeological Institute of America was founded and is run by classical scholars. Somewhat similarly, prehistory merges into protohistory and full history. More scholars have become general linguists coming from the various philologies than from anthropology. Culture history has been pursued also by historians and geographers, and some of the best has come from Sinologists. European folk ethnography is closest to what we call folklore, and in folklore students of English and other current languages of civilization are the more numerous. The result is that unless anthropologists are ethnographers, they share their specialty with collaborators in some natural science or in some humanity and are likely to be outnumbered by them.

What impulse is it that drives anthropologists as a group to participate in so many fields which are already being cultivated by others? It seems to be a two-prong impulse to apperceive and conceive at once empirically and holistically. We constitute one of the smaller learned professions, but we aim to take in perhaps more phenomenal territory than any other discipline. Our coverage must of necessity be somewhat thin. Yet it is rarely either vague or abstruse—we start with concrete facts which we sense to carry an interest, and we stick with them. Perhaps our coverage can fairly be called spotty; though without implication of being random, irrelevant, disconnected. If a whole is steadily envisaged, the relation of its fragments can be significant, provided the parts are specifically known and are specifically located within the totality. So the holistic urge is perhaps what is most characteristic of us.

This is balanced by a love of fact, an attachment to phenomena in themselves, to perceiving them through our own senses. This taproot we share with the humanities. And we also tend strongly here toward the natural history approach. Sociologists have called us "nature lovers" and "bird watchers," Steve Hart says; and from their angle, the epithets stick. There are anthropological museums of tangible objects, but no sociological ones. We are strong on photographs, films, and tapes that reproduce sights and sounds. We write chapters on art in ethnographies and sometimes offer courses in primitive art. How many sociologists would venture that, or even wish to venture it?

We insist on field work as an opportunity, a privilege, and a professional cachet. We want the face-to-face experience with our subjects. The anonymity of the sociological questionnaire seems to us bloodless, even though its specificity and quantification are obvious assets to which we cannot easily attain by our methods. When the Lynds went in person to study Middletown-Muncie, it was widely heralded as a taking-over of anthropological technique.

To return to the other prong of the bow, the holism, this seems expressed also in our inclination to historical and to comparative treatment. American sociology is certainly neither antihistorical nor anticomparative in principle; but it certainly is heavily interested in the here and now, in our own culture and social structure more often than in foreign, remote, or past ones. Sociology began with a marked ameliorative bent, and with concern for practical matters of utility. Anthropology commenced rather with an interest in the exotic and useless. We did not constitute our Society for Applied Anthropology until 1941. The "action research" of World War II was largely thrust upon us by government and military, and by many is remembered as a sort of spree of forced decision-making.

It is certainly significant that the sharing of anthropological fields is with the natural sciences and with the humanities. The only active overlap with any social science is that on theory with sociology. Specific primitive ethnography and most of the community studies in civilized societies continue to be done by anthropologists, quantifiable studies of problems in civilization by sociologists. The latter tend to define terms more sharply and problems more limitedly. They probably rank next to economists and psychologists in abundance of statistical treatment.

Balancing our virtual agreement on sociocultural theory, there exists, however, a strong drift in sociology to emphasize social structure and social action as compared with cultural product or pattern, and either to ignore the cultural accompaniments or to assume them as being somehow contained in or derivative from the social structure. Anthropologists, at any rate until recently, have contrariwise emphasized culture as their concern. To be sure they have made almost a fetish of kinship and have frequently given close attention to specific social aspects, ever since the initial days of Morgan and Bachofen. But they tend to look upon society as a part of domain of culture, on which one can specialize or not as one can specialize on religion or art or values, or again on subsistence, technology, and economics. Each procedure seems to give consistent results in the hands of those who follow it.

However, there is a point which no one seems yet to have thought quite through. Developmentally, evolutionistically, society far antedates and thus underlies culture, as shown by the existence of complex societies especially among insects, long before any culture existed. In man, who alone of all species substantially possesses culture, this invariably coëxists with society. In analytic study they are separable, and in practice one can focus on societies, or on cultures, or try to focus on the interrelations of the two. However, it remains conceptually unclear, at least to myself, how the sociologist can successfully treat culture as something in or derived from social structure, and the anthropologist can with equal success treat social structure as only a compartment or sector of culture. There is some legerdemain of words at work here, I feel, which my rational eye is not fast enough to perceive. I must admit I have found few colleagues who were seriously troubled by the contradiction that puzzles me.

I encounter a possibly related blocking of thought when I try to define "social anthropology" as a conscious movement or strand within total anthropology. It has emerged since my own maturity, as a successor to "functionalism," and the present generation of British social anthropologists have been trained by the "functionalists" Malinowski and Radcliffe-Brown. In Britain, where sociology is little recognized, social anthopologists stress the "social" aspect of their work and appear to accord primacy to social structure much as do American sociologists. At the same time they are obviously interested in cultures holistically, much as the rest of us are, and they are excellent ethnographers, as indeed Malinowski was when he did not let facile theorizing seduce him away from his superb descriptions of concrete culture functioning. But why the separatism, the limited circle?

In America social anthropology seems to have started with Lloyd Warner when he came back from Radcliffe-Brown in Australia. Warner is interested in the interactions of persons in society, especially our own, and perhaps most of all in social mobility. He uses cultural data skillfully to vivify his basically social-structural findings.

Perhaps the British are really still doing ethnography—reporting on culture—but are giving it additional *depth* by socializing it more than when Boas, Lowie, and I were doing field work. If so, the fact would take social anthropology out of the category of an exclusive cult, and would leave it as an endeavor at needed and vital enrichment of long-established cultural aims.

In that case "social anthropology" would resemble culture-and-personality, or personality-in-culture, which started out selfconsciously as a revolutionizing new dimension of anthropology, but seems now to be essentially adding greater depth of personalization

117

to the analysis of culture than was at first thought necessary, possible, or meet.

Since personalities are initially determined by their ancestry, it is highly relevant that anthropology was not a social science at all originally. Its father was natural science; its mother aesthetically tinged humanities. Both parents want to attain reasoned and general conclusions; but they both also want to reach them by way of their senses. After a brief first childlike decade of outright speculation, anthropology settled down to starting directly from experienced phenomena, with a bare minimum of ready-made abstraction and theory, but with a glowing conviction that it was entering new territory and making discovery. Its discovery was the world of culture, an enormous product and a vast influence, with forms and patterns of its own, and a validating principle: relativity. There were far boundaries to this demesne, which included in its totality alike our own and the most remote and diverse human productivities. The vision was wide, charged, and stirring. It may perhaps fairly be called romantic: certainly, it emerged historically about at the point when aesthetic romanticism was intellectualizing. The pursuit of anthropology must have seemed strange to many people; but no one has ever called it an arid or a dismal science.

Now, maturity has stolen upon us. The times, and utilitarianism, have caught up with us, and we find ourselves classified and assigned to the social sciences. It is a dimmer atmosphere, with the smog of jargon sometimes hanging heavy. Generalizations no longer suffice; we are taught to worship Abstraction; sharp sensory outlines have melted into vague ones. As our daily bread, we invent hypotheses in order to test them, as we are told is the constant practice of the high tribe of physicists. If at times some of you, like myself, feel ill at ease in the house of social science, do not wonder; we are changelings therein; our true paternity lies elsewhere.

I do *not* end on a note of despondency; for the routes of fulfillment are many. It is well that with all their differences of habitus, of attitude, of building stone, sociology and anthropology have emerged with a substantially common basic theory. That should be an encouragement to both; and a rallying point to others.

On Human Nature *

✤ Among cultureless or virtually cultureless animals, it is relatively easy to describe their characteristic behavior, just because it is practically unimpinged on by the highly variable factor of culture. A large component of their behavior is genetically founded, and, since physical environment tends to be stable and long-term, the effects of this environment have mostly been incorporated in the genetic constitution of the species through selection. The influence of organic environment or ecology has also been at least partly absorbed into the congenital make-up. The remainder of the organic environment is obviously, in a state of non-domestication, the principal factor which makes for individual learning.

The result is that we know pretty well the characteristic behavior patterns of bovines or felines, of chipmunks, porpoises, or elephants, of wrens and loons, of snakes and frogs. While reports by amateurs on the behavior of animals may often inject anthropomorphizing and dubious motivation, a mass of thoroughly reliable observation by zoölogists is also available. The behavior is the externally directed functioning corresponding to the animals' bodily structure. It bears obvious resemblance, greater or less, to human behavior and conditions, and is therefore construable—provisionally at least—in "psychological" terms. In some cases we can now infer which parts of the behavior are congenital and which individually learned. In others, the discrimination can be made by sufficient observation, properly directed; or if necessary, by test. We have therefore in hand or within reach a considerable body of objective knowledge on the behavioral "nature" of various animals: the essential and constant qualitative patterns of the psychological activity of many very different species.

By contrast with all subhuman species, in man the behavioral picture is enormously complicated by his possessing culture. Culture is of course based on a genetic endowment—indeed presumably a very special cerebral genetic endowment. But, viewed operatively, culture

* REPRINTED BY permission from *Southwestern Journal of Anthropology*, Vol. II, no. 3, pp. 195–204.

is supergenetic. It is acquired by learning from other individuals of the species, and is practiced and somewhat modified by each member of the human race individually; and his modifications enter into the continuum or joint product which is passed on to subsequent individuals. The chief mechanism which makes communication of human culture possible, and thereby makes culture possible, is the faculty of symbolization and speech. This faculty is hereditary: all normal human beings possess it to an adequate degree; other species possess it, at most only to a rudimentary degree. It is certainly the most fruitful in effects of all the specific characteristics of man; and it is difficult not to believe that the faculty must be the result of a genetic mutation or group of mutations.

Culture, including speech and symbol or idea systems, is individually acquired—"learned" by each individual from the other individuals he associates with. As these groups of associates or societies are spread in many parts and environments all over the earth, and as these have each had a more or less separate and different history, they show much diversity. This notorious plasticity or variability of human culture is due precisely to the fact that its content and forms, its substance, are non-genetic, and are therefore exempt from the overwhelmingly repetitive and preservative influence of heredity. The customs—which viewed systematically are the culture—of human societies often differ drastically; and their languages differ radically and totally—as much perhaps as orders, classes, or even phyla of animals, if such a comparison may be made by way of illustration. Yet in their organic morphology, the most divergent human societies are only races within the confines of one zoölogic species.

Owing to the largeness of this highly variable component of culture in the make-up of human behavior, it is evident that "human nature" is a much less steadily uniform thing, and much harder to characterize, than gorilla or elephant or tiger nature. Its hereditary features carry an enormous overlay of variable features due to culture. In fact, social psychologists and some sociologists often say that there is no human nature as such—only Chinese, Italian, Hottentot, etc. human nature. This seemingly absurd statement of course means only that generic human nature is so molded or distorted or reshaped by

Chinese culture in China and by Italian in Italy, that it nowhere occurs or is given as such; and this is a warning to naïve fellow-psychologists that they must not assume they are dealing with pan-human psychology when they are describing contemporary American behavior, no matter how refined their tests or statisticized their method.

Actually, of course, though it can not possibly anywhere be uncovered in its purity, original or pure human nature exists as a theoretically separable and essentially constant component in the Chinese, Italian, and the hundreds of other ethnic or social groups, which are fusion products of genetic, individual-accidental, and sociocultural influences.

While psychologists at least aim at universals, as they pervade individuals, the first focus of anthropologists is on specific features of groups, as that of historians is on specific events or on particular and even unique conditions. Anthropologists expect to deal primarily with human nature as it is expressed in the dress of particular cultures, and are not disturbed by its particularity as psychologists would be. As a matter of fact, for several decades they have been very little troubled by what generic human nature might be, because they had come to realize that it was far more constant than actual, culture-determined human nature; so much so that they would not be far in error if in the present state of precision or imprecision of their methods, they simply assumed, provisionally, that generic human nature was constant. At least they could assume it as averaging about constant for races and societies, though not for individuals; but then individuals are not their first professional concern.

Incidentally, historians, who are less theory-conscious even than anthropologists, have made and do *de facto* make the same assumption, whether they are aware of it or not, that human nature runs alike in all larger groups of men.

The earlier anthropologists, it is true—those who promulgated broad evolutionistic speculations beginning in the decade of the *Origin of Species*, and until as late as 1895–1915—far from discounting human nature as a factor profitably ignored, built on it. They were still, as in the early phases of many sciences, confident that they

121

were discovering unconditional universals, and progressive ones. And what was there better to derive their universals from than human nature? It was the basis and mainspring of all human action, individual and social; so institutions and beliefs just spontaneously grew out of it. Consequently beliefs and institutions in one place and another, at one time or another, tended to show a strong similarity. It was through accidents that they differed, and incidentally; in their important aspects they were similar—must be related because they all flowed out of human nature. Time and again Frazer in establishing a relationship or a sequence says: "What is more natural than that this should happen" or "that they did so and so." Frazer indeed strongly savored exotic practices and beliefs; but it was as seasoning of the steady monotony of a diet of universals that were an emanation of our nature.

Those easy, golden years of just dipping into the human nature of common experience to make anthropological science about primitives and origins are long since over. They were succeeded by the era of criticism and cultural relativism. As a result, it became apparent that human nature had not been defined; that it would be very difficult to characterize in all the Protean forms which it assumed; that it evidently was basically rather uniform; and that it could therefore be canceled out of our operations as a constant.

Now this period in turn is drawing to a close, and basic human nature is once more being felt as an existent. Bidney brings it into his *Theoretical Anthropology* of 1953; Spiro in a 1954 *American Anthropologist* article. It is a subject that is again being talked about by anthropologists; and it is clear that we cannot permanently ignore the basic genetic part of our psychology.

This essay then attempts to suggest some ways in which the problem of human nature may be grappled with.

It will, however, clarify this objective if we first eliminate some procedures that seem unfruitful.

First, we shall not learn to understand better what human nature is if we try to begin with a formal verbal definition of what is meant by human nature. Useful definitions come at the end of inquiry.

Second, inquiry must be systematic, utilizing the known results of previous scientific inquiry. This rules out any verbally more elaborate restatements of the commonplaces of common knowledge and common sense. It is not that these are without truth. But so do all proverbs contain truth, and yet scientific inquiry does not start from or operate with proverbs, be they overt or pedantically disguised.

Third, we may leave aside consideration of the "common denominators" of culture which have been several times proposed, exemplified, and even listed by anthropologists. Again, it is not that they are untrue; but they seem useless: no one has been able to develop the approach. I suspect the reason for this sterility to be that the emphasizing of common denominators is at bottom an endeavor to define human nature from culture, to deduce it from culture; which is open to objection equal to that of deriving culture from human nature. The two procdeures might be described as inverse forms of reductionism.

The same holds for the "universal pattern" of culture, that seed lightly tossed out by Wissler that has never germinated. Once more, the concept is not untrue; but an enumerative table of contents, while useful in its place, is not a productive tool for research.

Finally, we shall rule out "needs," including needs that appear under new names. Basically, they also are commonplaces of common knowledge. If elaborated, they are usually psychological restatements of cultural behavior.

There may be several approaches toward the problem of defining human nature, but I discern only two with any specificity. There are abundant data available for both; but the data need more systematic examination from the angle of our particular problem. Before we attain new results it may be necessary to assemble additional facts, or to recheck or reinterpret some of those on hand. But the first step would seem to be a comprehensive and systematic shaking down, from our point of view, of what there is in hand.

The first approach is intraspecific and cultural; the second, comparative and biological.

The approach through culture is simple. It would aim to delimit the perimeters of historic human culture, as established by the most extreme expressions yet found in particular cultures, of the various activities and qualities of culture. It is not to be expected that this delimitation would *per se* lead to any profoundly novel discoveries. It would be an organized stock taking, a systematic review from one angle. But the limits of human culture, both normal limits and extreme ones, are presumably set mainly if not wholly by the normal and extreme limits of congenital human nature. And such a delimitation of the expressions of human nature would at least be a first step toward defining our problem by including as well as excluding those phenomena presumably most relevant to human nature. It might be at least the beginning of an escape from the mishmash of common and inexact knowledge, common and dilettante speculation, and unrealized hangovers from religious and ethical systems, that make up our present thinking or talking about human nature.

An exemplification of "most extreme expressions" is human sacrifice as practiced by the ancient Mexicans; or frequency of cannibalism among certain Polynesians and Melanesians. In completeness, intensity, and variety of asceticism I presume the inhabitants of India have gone farthest, as they certainly have in intensity, variety, and non-residualness of hiearchical grouping in castes, and—along with the Tibetans—in institutionalized polyandry. In the realm of thought, first place would presumably also go to India both for philosophical pessimism and for love of classification on its own account. India is of course mentioned only for convenience of identification: it is the cultural manifestation that is the relevant material, not the place or people.

The Japanese forty-seven ronins would perhaps serve as an extreme of institutionalized loyalty. For pervasive cleanliness, neatness, order, finish, and restrictive elimination of physical superfluities, the Japanese would again come strongly into consideration; for going without artifacts, tools, and property, the Australian natives.

These examples may suffice to make my meaning clear. I have deliberately avoided citing any from Western civilization for fear of bias in perspective and evaluation where there is participation.

Even brief consideration of this topic seems to indicate that certain cultures, such as the Chinese, will be represented but rarely at the perimeter of pan-human extremity; others of equal size and weight of

achievement, such as the Indian, repeatedly. The theoretical pre-
eminence accorded the sage and priest over the ruler; the propensity
toward the abstract, the priority allowed the conceptual over the
sensory, the addiction to exaggeration and absolutes, are further cases
in point from India. Followed up systematically, this side line of frequency evaluation should result in a rating of cultures on a scale of
centering respectively well in the interior or toward the rim of the
total range of human culture (and therefore human nature, presumably); or perhaps of nearness to different segments of the perimeter.
This is of course not part of the problem of human nature as such,
but it might be a by-product of the proposed line of investigation.
But even as an avowed distraction this side issue serves to show how
much more readily problems loom into sight when a field is viewed for
a time from one consistent angle than when it is viewed indetermi-
nately from several.

Incidentally, if this suggested side line proved productive, it seems
that the differential placing of disparate cultures within the perimeter
of total human culture and total human nature might also contribute
to the definition and characterization of the "modal personality" of
these cultures.

At any rate, total human culture viewed historically and comparatively—cross-culturally is the modern word—obviously must essentially coincide with human nature from which it grows; and its perimeter being therefore the perimeter of human nature, this definable
coincidence suggests itself as an opportune toe hold from which to
start further inquiry into human nature. I do not know where else
in the range of the two aspects, than at the periphery, we can allege
any point-for-point correspondence of their phenomena.

It is true that potential human nature almost certainly has a
slightly wider range than the sum total of known culture expressions.
The perimeter of recorded culture would therefore fall within that
of the potential nature. But—one thing at a time; and it is unprofit-
able to think too much about what extensions or revisions of understanding the future may or may not bring.

It will be seen that the proposal is opposite to the method of
Frazer and the former cultural evolutionists. Basically, they "ex-

plained"—actually, derived—certain of the more or less known phenomena of culture from the more immediately but less definitely known nature of man. I am proposing to start from the limits of known culture in the hope of finding somewhat better understanding of the undifferentiated magma of human psychic constitution.

The second approach would be a somewhat analogous inventory and methodical survey, among subhuman animals, of behavior patterns similar to or anticipatory of human cultural behavior patterns. This survey would be comparative between man and other animals; and between definitely culturally expressed patterns and predominantly congenital or individually learned patterns. These last two ingredients, the congenital (genetic) and the individually learned, should of course be distinguished whenever possible. But the distinction is not always easy at present; and when it cannot be made, the two could still be legitimately and perhaps profitably compared jointly with human culture—which is also learned and which also expresses, however variably, a congenital constitution, but which is acquired socially and symbolically.

For instance, it is widely maintained that an element of play or playfulness enters into human and therefore cultural aesthetic, intellectual, and perhaps religious activities. A sound and critical review of the nature and range of play in the animal kingdom as well as its absences, based only on sound biological data and interpretation, would supply a firmer foundation for our understanding of the "value segment" of human culture. It might even react back on biological interpretation.

The diversity of play behavior, as between phyla, classes, and even orders, is astonishing. It may be questioned whether any invertebrates play except as part of mating. The same may hold for the cold-blooded vertebrates; but scraps of exception would be most interesting. Warm-blooded mammals play mostly in youth, but warm-blooded birds never in youth. Even adult courtship play in birds tends toward intensity and seriousness. Nonsexual play is largely confined to a few families, such as crows and magpies and parrots.

Among mammals there are enormous differences. Insectivores and rodents play little; seals and whales possibly most of all.

Primates vary—compare baboons and chimpanzees. If they play, it seems to be with accompaniment of unusual affect. Carnivores on the whole play more than herbivores; but there are contraries, such as the elephant on one side, and weasels and minks on the other. Some carnivores play until almost old age: raccoons and otters especially. The corresponding raptorial birds are playless, except for a few courtship flights.

There are many purely biological problems unsolved in this area, especially as regards correlates of greater or less playfulness: size, diet, medium inhabited, protection and sustenance provided the young, and so forth.

This extraordinary organic and phylogenetic diversity has a striking analogue in the diversity and plasticity of those sectors of culture supposedly embodying expressions or sublimations of play impulses—the "value segment" of culture already mentioned. This may be mere coincidence; but it also suggests that systematized comparison might be fruitful—even on both sides of the line that separates the organic from the organic-plus.

It seems unnecessary at this stage to do more than enumerate some of the further topics that would be relevant.

The now notorious pecking-order and the whole realm of inter-individual dominance suggest much in human social and political institutions.

The societal aspects of animal life are of course of primary importance because human societies are a precondition of human cultures. Moreover socialization is one human property that has been developed to a definitely higher degree and greater integration among subhuman bees, ants, and termites—which possess only exceedingly rudimentary traces of culture. It is probably significant that this inverse weighting occurs among the arthropods, a phylum very different from our own. There is excellent literature both on the social insects and on animal aggregations and societies in general, but it has not been adequately exploited by sociocultural studies.

The "schooling" of fishes (and birds in flight, etc.) is related to sociality but with special emphasis on kinaesthetic phenomena, and has obvious counterparts in culture and human social psychology.

Behavior related to ownership is most developed on the subhuman level with reference to space—the individual "territoriality" of many birds and some mammals and fishes. Much but not all of it is related to nesting, breeding, brooding, and nurture of the young. Certainly territorial ownership is far more widely spread, intense, and functionally significant in the subhuman area than all other kinds of ownership. Linton may therefore have been right in suggesting that human concern for property is an outgrowth of sense of territoriality. Curiously, the nonhuman primates seem to manifest rather little attachment to either places or objects.

Possessiveness toward objects has a very spotty subhuman occurrence—the presenting and stealing of pebbles by penguins, the thefts of shiny objects by crows and magpies, the hoarding of almost anything unusual by packrats, etc. Most warm-blooded species and even families seem to lack such behavior altogether; and so do probably all cold-blooded animals. When the trait does occur, its functional relevance seems weak, as if it were a selectively non-significant spillover or "perversion" or residue from mating, breeding, home-building or food-storing patterns. It might also represent something like congenital aesthetic appreciativeness.

Home building ranges all the way from automatic secretions remaining adherent to the invertebrate body, through spun covers, cases, or webs, to elaborate constructions of extrasomatic materials by some birds and beavers. The structures may be individual or social; their function, protection of the individual or the offspring or the group. There is no close correlation with degree of total advancement: ants chiefly burrow or excavate, termites build with excretions, bees with secretions, some wasps with gathered mud or masticated cellulose. Most fish are homeless, some merely wave out a hollow or clearing for their young, but the subfish lampreys carry stones to their spawning place. Among mammals, rodents often both burrow and assemble bedding as well as storing food; carnivores may burrow; ungulates generally do nothing at all and are homeless; a few primates make gestures toward a nest of half-broken or bent branches. The prevalence of nest building among non-running birds is obviously associated with holding the eggs together during brooding and the fledglings during feeding, as well as with protection. As might be expected, nest building and a sense of territoriality show a strong correlation.

Nests and structures of extrasomatic materials are of course artifacts. Beyond "housing," however, artifacts are definitely rare on the subhuman level; and so is gathering or storage of anything else than food. There are a few cases of extrasomatic uses of "tools," such as wasps tamping with pebbles, finches holding broken-off thorns to spear insects in crevices, monkeys picking up and hurling missiles. A systematic and critical evaluation of these few cases of subcultural tools might be illuminating. So would be a comparative listing of all materials, both somatic and extrasomatic, utilized extrasomatically.

Finally there are the two important fields of dance, rhythmic play, song, noise for its own sake—in short, the field of the arts in culture —and of "communication" in the wider sense—signals, sentinels, "teaching," etc. Here the findings of the von Frisch group on bee communications are outstanding and hold hope both of more results to come and of extension to other families and orders. The imitative song and speech of parrots, mynahs, mockingbirds, etc. presumably participate in both "art" and "communication," and have a further relevance of their own in that the feature of copying makes them cases of learning from the outset. If these birds learn from members of their own species as readily as from individuals of other species, as is likely but seems not proved, we have indubitable tradition at work; and therewith culture, at least of a kind. I say "of a kind" because it serves no apparent survival function, direct or indirect, but seems a matter of random amusement, playful exercise, and fitful by-products. Could it be that human culture had its first origins in analogous trivialities, and only gradually developed its seriousness and major potentialities? If not, what is the philosophic and genetic relation of the aimless and sterile "culture" of these tradition-imitating bird species to our culture? The questions are cited as illustrations of the sort of problems that the comparative subhuman inventory suggested might raise or even answer.

Similarly stimulating might be a list of behaviors that occur universally in human societies and cultures but seem universally lacking in subhuman species. Such would be: knowledge of death, concern with the future, the incest restriction, religion, extra-somatic visual art, verbal or muscular expressions of humor. Some of these might have to be modified or withdrawn, but others would presumably be added. As the inventory consolidated and grew it might well suggest new and more precise perspectives on what factors subhuman organic evolution and human cultural evolution possessed in common and differentially.

I keep referring to inventory, review, stock taking because I believe there is a vast body of observations, a large proportion of them critical and sound, of natural history type in the fullest scientific sense of that term, which tend to seem largely of marginal significance to most biologists as they pursue their daily work, and which anthropologists are to an even greater extent too preoccupied to utilize. In fact, the segment of anthropologists that have entered the profession from the social science side are for the most part profoundly ignorant of this class of phenomena.

I am not advocating experiment, which is difficult and too easily lets its own technique overshadow results. The value of experiment, which isolates a situation from its context in nature, is at critical points *after* these have been determined. Psychologists with rats in mazes presumably know the critical points in their problems, which I take to be theoretical and definitional, not intrinsically comparative and certainly not historical. The series of problems to which my foregoing suggestions refer are broadly historical, being concerned with evolution—the relation of cultural history to organic history. No doubt there are critical points in this field which can ultimately be clinched by experiment—von Frisch and Lorenz have demonstrated this—but the first need is for sifting of the accumulated observations to sharpen the focus on what is critical. What I have done in the preceding pages is to try to suggest some of the considerations which might guide such sifting.

That absorption of the data is the first requisite is something I feel certain of. Knowledge, factual knowledge, descriptive knowledge of form and of behavior, is what Darwin accumulated for twenty years after he found the concept of natural selection; and it enabled him in a few months to write *The Origin of Species* and establish evolution in the stream of modern thought.

I should love to participate in the adventure that I envisage and have outlined; but I must pass on the opportunity to younger bodies.

Selected Bibliography

1909 The Archaeology of California. In: *Putnam Anniversary Volume. Anthropological Essays Presented to Frederic Ward Putnam in Honor of His Seventieth Birthday, April 16, 1909, by His Friends and Associates* (New York, G. E. Stechert), pp. 1–42.

1909 The Bannock and Shoshoni Languages. *American Anthropologist*, n.s., 11(2):266–77.

1909 Notes on Shoshonean Dialects of Southern California. *University of California Publications in American Archaeology and Ethnology*, 8(5): 235–69.

1910 Contributions to *Handbook of American Indians North of Mexico* (N–Z), ed. by Frederick Webb Hodge. *Bulletin of Bureau of American Ethnology*, no. 30, part II.

1912 Ishi, the Last Aborigine. *World's Work Magazine*, 24(3):304–8.

1912 The Determination of Linguistic Relationship. *Anthropos*, 8(2):389–401.

1915 Eighteen Professions. *American Anthropologist*, n.s., 17(3):283–88.

1916 Arapaho Dialects. *University of California Publications in American Archaeology and Ethnology*, 12(3):71–138.

1916 California Place Names of Indian Origin. *University of California Publications in American Archaeology and Ethnology*, 12(2):31–69.

1916 The Speech of a Zuñi Child. *American Anthropologist*, n.s., 18(4): 529–34.

1916 Zuñi Potsherds. *Anthropological Papers of American Museum of Natural History*, 18 (pt. 1):i–ii, 1–37.

1917 California Kinship Systems. *University of California Publication in American Archaeology and Ethnology*, 12(9):339–96.

1917 The Superorganic. *American Anthropologist*, n.s., 19(2):163–213.

1917 Zuñi Kin and Clan. *Anthropological Papers of American Museum of Natural History*, 18(pt. II):i–ii, 39–204.

1918 Heredity, Environment and. Civilization. *American Museum Journal*, 18(5):351–59.

1918 The History of Philippine Civilization as Reflected in Religious Nomenclature. *Anthropological Papers of American Museum of Natural History*, 19(pt. II): i–ii, 35–67.

1918 The Possibility of a Social Psychology. *American Journal of Sociology*, 23(5):633–50.

1919 On the Principle of Order in Civilization as Exemplified by Changes of Fashion. *American Anthropologist*, n.s., 21(3):235–63.

1919 Peoples of the Philippines. *American Museum of Natural History. Handbook Series*, no. 8. 224 pp.

1920 California Culture Provinces. *University of California Publications in American Archaeology and Ethnology*, 17(2):i–ii, 151–69.

1920 Totem and Taboo: An Ethnologic Psychoanalysis. *American Anthropologist*, n.s., 22 (1):48–55.

1920 Yuman Tribes of the Lower Colorado. *University of California Publications in American Archaeology and Ethnology*, 16(8):475–85.

1921 Indians of Yosemite. In: *Handbook of Yosemite National Park*, compiled and ed. by Ansel F. Hall (New York, and London, Putnam), pp. 51–73.

1921 Observation on the Anthropology of Hawaii. *American Anthropologist*, n.s. 23(2):221–22.

1922 Elements of Culture in Native California. *University of California Publications in American Archaeology and Ethnology*, 13(8):259–328.

1923 American Culture and the Northwest Coast. *American Anthropologist*, n.s., 25(1):1–20.

1923 *Anthropolgy*. New York, Harcourt, Brace. x + 523 pp.

1923 The History of Native Culture in California. *University of California Publications in American Archaeology and Ethnology*, 20:125–42.

1924 *Handbook of the Indians of California*. Bulletin, Bureau of American Ethnology, no. 78. Washington. xviii + 995 pp.

1924 Archaic Culture Horizons in the Valley of Mexico. *University of California Publications in American Archaeology and Ethnology*, 17(7):i–ii, 373–408.

1926 Archaeological Explorations in Peru. Part I, Ancient Pottery from Trujillo. *Anthropology Memoirs, Field Museum Natural History*, 2(1):1–44.

1927 Arrow Release Distributions. *University of California Publications in American Archaeology and Ethnology*, 23(4):i–ii, 283–96.

1927 Coast and Highland in Prehistoric Peru. *American Anthropologist*, n.s., 29(4):625–53.

1927   Disposal of the Dead. *American Anthropologist*, n.s., 29(3):308–15.

1927   *The Superorganic*. Hanover, Minneapolis, Liverpool, The Sociological Press. 37 pp. (Reprinted, with revisions, from *American Anthropologist*, 19(2), 1917.)

1928   The Anthropological Attitude. *American Mercury*, 13(52):490–96.

1928   Native Culture of the Southwest. *University of California Publications in American Archaeology and Ethnology*, 23(9):i–ii, 375–98.

1928   Sub-human Culture Beginnings. *Quarterly Review of Biology*, 3(3): 325–42.

1929   The Valley Nisenan. *University of California Publications in American Archaeology and Ethnology*, 24:(4):i, 253–90.

1930   Archaeology. In: *Encyclopedia of the Social Sciences*, ed. Edwin R. A. Seligman (New York, Macmillan), 2, 163–67.

1930   Art, Primitive. In: *Encyclopedia of the Social Sciences*, ed. Edwin R. A. Seligman (New York, Macmillan), 2, 163–67.

1930   Caste. In: *Encyclopedia of the Social Sciences*, ed. Edwin R. A. Seligman New York, Macmillan), 3, 254–57.

1930   Cultural Relations between North and South America. *Proceedings 23d International Congress of Americanists, held at New York*, pp. 5–22.

1931   Historical Reconstruction of Culture Growths and Organic Evolution. *American Anthropologist*, n.s., 33(2):149–56.

1932   With Harold Edson Driver. Quantitative Expression of Cultural Relationships. *University of California Publications in American Archaeology and Ethnology*, 31(4):i–ii, 211–56.

1933   Process in the Chinese Kinship System. *American Anthropologist*, n.s., 35(1):151–57.

1934   Blood-group Classification. *American Journal of Physical Anthropology*, 18(3):377–93.

1934   Cultural Anthropology. In: *The Problem of Mental Disorder; a Study Undertaken by the Committee on Psychiatric Investigations, National Research Council*, Madison Bentley, Chairman (New York, and London, McGraw-Hill), pp. 346–53.

1934   Native American Population. *American Anthropologist*, n.s. 36(1):1–25.

1935   Preface. In: *Culture Element Distributions: I. The Structure of California Indian Culture*, by Stanislaw Klimek, *University of California Publications in American Archaeology and Ethnology*, 37(1):1–11.

1936   Prospects in California Prehistory. *American Antiquity*, 2(2):108–16.

1937   Archaeological Explorations in Peru. Part IV. Cañete Valley. *Anthropology Memoirs, Field Museum of Natural History*, 2(4):219–73.

1938   Basic and Secondary Patterns of Social Structure. *Journal of Royal Anthropological Institute of Great Britain and Ireland*, 68:299–309.

1939   Cultural and Natural Areas of Native North America. *University of California Publications in American Archaeology and Ethnology*, 38: xii + 242 pp. (Also issued in hard covers as a separate book.)

Alfred Kroeber

1939   Totem and Taboo in Retrospect. *American Journal of Sociology*, 45(3): 446–51.

1940   Conclusions: The Present Status of Americanistic Problems. The Maya and Their Neighbors. In: *Essays in Honor of Alfred Marston Tozzer*, ed. by Clarence L. Hay and others (New York, and London, Appleton), pp. 460–89.

1940   With Jane Richardson. Three Centuries of Women's Dress Fashions; a Quantitative Analysis. *Anthropological Records*, 5(2):i–iv, 111–53.

1943   Review of *A Study of History*, by Arnold J. Toynbee. *American Anthropologist*, n.s., 45(2):294–99.

1944   *Configurations of Culture Growth*. Berkeley and Los Angeles, University of California Press, x + 882 pp.

1946   *The Ancient* Oikoumené *as an Historic Culture Aggregate*. Huxley Memorial Lecture of 1945. The Royal Anthropological Institute of Great Britain and Ireland, London, 12 pp.

1946   The Chibcha. In: *Handbook of South American Indians*. Vol. 2. *The Andean Civilizations*, J. H. Steward, ed., *Bulletin Bureau of American Ethnology*, no. 143, pp. 887–909.

1947   My Faith. *The American Weekly*, April 6, p. 33.

1948   *Anthropology; Race, Language, Culture, Psychology, Prehistory*, new ed., rev. (New York, Harcourt, Brace), xii + 856 + xxxix pp.

1948   Summary and Interpretations. In: *A Reappraisal of Peruvian Archaeology*, assembled by Wendell C. Bennett, *Memoirs of Society of American Archaeology*, no. 4, pp. 113–21.

1949   Art. In: *Handbook of South American Indians, Vol. 5. The Comparative Ethnology of South American Indians*. J. H. Steward, ed., *Bulletin, Bureau of American Ethnology*, no. 143, pp. 411–92.

1949   Values as a Subject of Natural Science Inquiry. *Proceedings National Academy of Science*, 35(6):261–64.

1951   Is Western Civilization Disintegrating or Reconstituting? *Proceedings, American Philosophical Society*, 95(2):100–4.

1951   Social Anthropology: Past and Present. *Man*, 51(article 33):18.

1951   The Viking Fund and Anthropology. *The First Ten Years, 1941–1951*, including a report on the Fund's activities for the year ending January 31, 1951 (New York, The Viking Fund, Inc.), pp. 4–12.

1952   Acculturation in the Americas (address of greeting by the President of the Congress). In: *Proceedings and Selected Papers of the XXIXth International Congress of Americanists*, ed. by Sol Tax (Chicago, University of Chicago Press), pp. 12–14.

1952   With Clyde Kay Maben Kluckhohn. Culture; a Critical Review of Concepts and Definitions. With the assistance of Wayne Untereiner and appendices by Alfred G. Meyer. *Papers of the Peabody Museum of American Archaeology and Ethnology*, 47(1):i–viii, 224 (iv).

1952   *The Nature of Culture*. Chicago, University of Chicago Press, x + 438 pp.

1953 Concluding Review. In: *An Appraisal of Anthropology Today,* ed. by Sol Tax, Loren C. Eiseley, Irving Rouse, and Carl F. Vogelin (Chicago, University of Chicago Press), pp. 357–76.

1953 Discussion in: *An Appraisal of Anthropology Today,* ed. by Sol Tax, Loren C. Eiseley, Irving Rouse, and Carl F. Vogelin (Chicago, University of Chicago Press), pp. 39–40, 45, 47, 50, 60–61, 66, 118–19, 143–44, 151–52, 222, 280–81.

1954 The Place of Anthropology in Universities. *American Anthropologist,* 56(5):764–67.

1955 History of Anthropological Thought. In: *Yearbook of Anthropology—1955,* ed. by William L. Thomas, Jr. (New York, Wenner-Gren Foundation for Anthropological Research), pp. 293–311.

1957 *Style and Civilizations.* (Ithaca, N.Y., Cornell University Press.) vii + 191 pp.

1959 Ethnographic Interpretations, 7–11. *University of California Publications in American Archaeology and Ethnology,* 47(3):i–iv, 235–310.

1959 The Subject Matter of Anthropology. In: *Readings in Anthropology,* ed. by Morton H. Fried, *Vol. I, Readings in Physical Anthropology, Linguistics, and Archaeology* (New York, Crowell), pp. 3–5.

1960 Evolution, History and Culture. In: *Evolution after Darwin Vol. II, The Evolution of Man; Man, Culture and Society,* ed. by Sol Tax (Chicago, University of Chicago Press), pp. 1–16.

1960 On Typological Indices I: Ranking of Languages. *International Journal of American Linguistics,* 26(3):171–77.

1960 Selections in: *The Golden Age of American Anthropology,* sel. and ed. with introduction and notes by Margaret Mead and Ruth L. Bunzel (New York, Braziller), x + 630 pp.

1960 The Nature of Culture, pp. 478–84. (*Anthropology,* 1948, pp. 252–56, 288–90.)

1960 Statistics, Indo-European and Taxonomy. *Language,* 36(1):1–21.

1961 Semantic Contribution of Lexicostatistics. *International Journal of Linguistics,* 27(1):1–8.

1962 A Roster of Civilizations and Culture. An Essay on the Natural History of the World's Cultures, Living and Extinct. (Chicago, Aldine.) 96 pp.

137